race

an anthology

Crown Trade Paperbacks
New York

race

in the first person

edited by

bart
schneider

Grateful acknowledgment is given to the following photographers for permission to reprint their photographs: Michael Dorris: Louise Erdrich   Gerald Early: Washington University Photographic Services © 1994   Henry Louis Gates, Jr.: Jerry Bauer   Ira Glasser: Bob Adelman © 1991   Jessica Hagedorn: Karen Dacker   Russell Leong: Tsung Woo Han © 1996 Audre Lorde: Salimah Ali   Peggy McIntosh: Courtesy of Margaret Means McIntosh   Bharati Mukherjee: Jerry Bauer   Naomi Shahib Nye: Amy Arbus © 1995   John Powell: Tim Rummelhoff © 1993   Adrienne Rich: Gypsy P. Ray   Luis J. Rodríguez: Elan Photography Studios   Richard Rodriguez: Brit Thurston © 1992   Leslie Marmon Silko: Robyn McDaniels © 1992   Susan Straight: Susan Rae Lakin   John Edgar Wideman: News Office, University of Massachusetts   Cecil B. Williams: Alain McLaughlin © 1995

A complete listing of permissions to reprint previously published material appears on page vi.

Published by Crown Trade Paperbacks, 201 East 50th Street, New York, New York 10022. Member of the Crown Publishing Group.

Random House, Inc. New York, Toronto, London, Sydney, Auckland

http://www.randomhouse.com/

Crown Trade Paperbacks and colophon are trademarks of Crown Publishers, Inc.

Printed in the United States of America

Design by Jane Treuhaft

Library of Congress Cataloging-in-Publication Data
Race, an anthology in the first person / [edited by] Bart Schneider. — 1st ed.
        p.   cm.
    1. Minorities—United States.   2. Racism—United States.
    3. United States—Race relations.
    E184.A1R226   1997
    305.8'00973—dc20   96-23665
                                                  CIP

ISBN 0-517-88728-2 (pbk.)

10 9 8 7 6 5 4 3 2 1

First Edition

for patricia

wise woman who has taught me kindness

acknowledgments

I am indebted to the staff of the *Hungry Mind Review*, past and present, without whom this collection would not exist. A special thanks to Margaret Todd Maitland, who it is my great pleasure to work with year after year. Thanks for both your practical wisdom and fierce imagination. Thanks to Martha Davis Beck for your high spirit, intelligence, and guiding enthusiasm; to Diana Katigbak BenJafaar, the keeper of humor and wisdom, and a soulful pulse on reality; to Andy Nelson for your humanity and for keeping us looking so good; to Pieter Martin for reading all the magazines in the Western world and keeping me awake with your reports; to David Unowsky for giving me the chance, even though you might not have realized the mess you were getting yourself into; to Laura Etherton for your wit and for the great cover; to Sam Haselby for your tireless intelligence and for challenging me more than I sometimes wanted; to Philip Patrick for your bottomless imagination and deep friendship; to Emily Bloch for bringing such graceful order to the minutia of this enterprise.

Thank you to John Kostishack for helping me understand that whites cannot be impervious to race; to john powell for your clarity, inspiration, and friendship; to Ruth Elizabeth Burks for your invaluable help with the questionnaire; to Fiona McCrae for helping me see the shape of this collection; to Susan Bergholz for your sage advice; to Samuel L. Meyers, Jr., and Judy Leahy of the Roy Wilkins Center for Human Relations and Social Justice for taking *Hungry Mind Review*'s race project seriously; to Nicole Aragi, jazz buddy and agent, and Eliza Scott, sushi freak and editor, for believing in this project. Thanks.

contents

introduction

A few years ago civil rights attorney Lani Guinier called for a national conversation about race, but the political leadership declined the invitation. For white politicians, race has become either a hot potato, or the centerpiece in a politics of fear. One can argue that President Clinton's silence on race is little improvement over George Bush's demonizing of blacks in his 1992 reelection campaign ads featuring Willie Horton, or Pat Buchanan's shouted mantra at the Mexican border: "Jose, we ain't gonna let you in again!"

What's going on here? Are whites planning to "circle the wagons" now that the majority of America's population is no longer white? The spirit of the Great Society and Civil Rights era of the sixties and seventies has crumbled, and an enormous vacuum exists: white political leaders who'd normally stand up against the demonization of "the other" have gone fishing. More worrisome, the "white vacuum" is reflected in the lives of once idealistic boomers. Have they all moved to the suburbs?

In May 1994, in that rarefied age before O.J., the magazine I edit, *Hungry Mind Review*, published an extensive questionnaire probing people's attitudes, beliefs, and personal experience on the subject of race, in advance of a planned issue devoted to the subject. In the next months, close to a thousand handwritten and typed responses poured into our office. Our readers, a large majority of whom are white and college educated, filled out the questionnaire with a surprising rigor. I had the image of a small mass of men and women, huddled over kitchen counters, scratching away at their thoughts about race.

Because the questionnaire (which is included in this volume at the back) starts by asking readers to take a retrospective look at how their views on race have been formed, many readers claimed that in answering they relived a small part of their childhood. And some were shocked to realize that they had been taught, through words or allusion, that blacks and Latinos were lazy, were inferior, were to be feared.

"It is hard to be honest about this," one reader wrote, "because of the shame I feel over being so *basic*. Somewhere in my life, probably as a child, I was given the thought that 'they' would take over. I do not know who 'they' are and suspect they are anybody who is not 'us.' We are white."

Some mornings, after we brought in the mail, a dozen soul-searching responses spilled out of envelopes and our funky office-in-a-little-house would seem like a bizarre confessional, a national clearing house for anonymous souls to reveal their views about race. I kept thinking, hey if nobody in this country wants to talk about race, how come we keep getting so much mail?

One question provoked a stunning, if not surprising, polarity of answers—How important is race to your sense of self? Many white readers regarded race as a peripheral part of their identity, whereas black, Latino, and Asian readers were unequivocal in declaring race as central to their identity. Some whites seemed to wear their imperviousness to race as a badge of virtue. They were above race, they weren't prejudiced at all, they couldn't see what all the fuss was about. Others wrote elaborate narratives about their racial histories that reminded me of the guy who goes to the shrink for the sole purpose of confirming that he doesn't need to be there.

As a white man, I've long enjoyed the privilege of choosing whether or not to regard race as relevant, and I have been slow to understand the luxury of having the choice. I was frightened when faced with devoting an issue of the *Hungry Mind Review* to race. On the surface, I was afraid to be entering a messy territory in which it seemed nothing useful could be said. My greater fear was that in facing racial inequities, I would ultimately be faced with myself and a choice between acting or retreating to an area of greater comfort. This is where the conversation begins for me.

This collection, which grows out of *Hungry Mind Review*'s Race issue, presents some of America's finest contemporary writers and social leaders exploring race in a range of first person idioms, from essays and memoirs to letters and sermons.

The power of the first person voice that drives this collection is in its directness and simplicity. It's you talking to me, me to you. It's Reverend Cecil Williams preaching to hundreds on a Sunday morning in Glide Church in San Francisco: "Sometimes people will ask me: Where'd you get all that hope? . . . I know this—that the human condition can always have hope where two or three are gathered together." It's Audre Lorde speaking to a woman's conference in Connecticut: "My response to racism is anger. . . . My anger has meant pain to me, but it has also meant survival, and before I give it up I'm going to be sure that there is something at least as powerful to replace it on the road to clarity." It's John Wideman talking in letter and in spirit to his son in prison: "I hope this is not a hard day for you. I hope you can muster peace within yourself and deal with the memories. . . ." Listening closely to the human voice can keep us human.

To approach a territory as freighted with suffering and shame, guilt and indifference, rhetoric and amnesia, with passionate personal testimony is to stake a claim, to demand a place in which we can talk to each other about who we are and what we hope America might one day become.

Finally, it seems to me, that race gives way, in the pieces collected here, to a universal yearning for justice and power, a justice and power that also involves class and gender. In her essay "White Privilege: Unpacking the Invisible Knapsack," Peggy McIntosh tells us that "To make systems equitable we need first to acknowledge their colossal unseen dimensions. The silences and denials surrounding privilege are the key. . . . It is not a matter for blame or guilt. We did not ask to be born into these systems. But having seen them, we can if we wish take some responsibility for using unearned power to share power."

BART SCHNEIDER
April 1996

gerald
early
susan
straight

I
home place

henry
louis
gates, jr.
naomi
shihab
nye
jessica
hagedorn
michael
dorris
richard
rodriguez

gerald early

gerald
early

Gerald Early, born in 1952, grew up in Philadelphia. A graduate of the University of Pennsylvania and Cornell University, Early is a professor of English and African-American Studies at Washington University. *Tuxedo Junction*, his first collection of essays, was awarded the Giles Whiting Prize, and his second collection, *The Culture of Bruising*, won the 1995 National Book Critics Circle Award in Criticism. Other recent books include a meditation on Motown, *One Nation Under a Groove* and *Daughters: On Family and Fatherhood*, a personal examination of family life.

Early's natural form seems to be the free-ranging cultural essay. His essays travel through a stunning series of locales, from prizefighting rings and Weight Watchers' meetings to campus debates about Malcolm X, and to his peculiar spot in front of the television watching Shirley Temple movies with his daughters. That Early has become one of America's most important cultural critics is due, in part, to his ability to explore contradictions within the culture as well as within himself. He is a freethinker, a man who has not made up his mind in advance, and who is never comfortable adopting the party line.

Gerald Early lives with his wife and two daughters in Saint Louis.

the american mysticism of remembrance

AN INSTANCE OF STORYTELLING

> *And the day came on which I was actually to be freed of*
> *this profession of rhetoric . . .*
> —ST. AUGUSTINE, *Confessions*, Book IX, Chapter 4

For any thinking black person, one of the more remarkable, if not comforting, features of the month of February in recent years (with the celebration of black history being something of the rage in an otherwise gloomy season unless we have a Persian Gulf war going on) is not only that one is reminded of the race burden with more force than usual but that one is also forced to deal with the burden of an untenable history, a common American preoccupation. There is something about Black History Month (now at least six weeks long, as Martin Luther King's birthday celebration in mid-January gives us an early start on the festivities) that seems alternately depressing, even crushing, and (at least in some small way) strangely moral and necessary—although the ethical imperative of this quaint American institution can barely justify the sheer pedestrian and mediocre insistence of its being. One is always caught between taking it too seriously and wanting to laugh at it as something of a very bad joke that can be funny only in America, where the "punch line," so to speak, is both so obvious and so pathetic. There is only so much of this sort of dementia, so much of this rampant intellectual trivialization generated by guilt, that this culture can stand.

My earliest memories of Black History Month are from the late

1950s and early 1960s, when I was an elementary school student. Then it was Negro History Week, so named by its inventor the black historian, Harvard Ph.D., and committed "race man" Carter G. Woodson back in 1926, about ten years after he founded the Association for the Study of Negro Life and History. My black teachers (I attended a nearly all-black grade school), nearly all of whom were products of black schools like Cheney State, Morgan State, Hampton, Fisk, and the like, taught us, predictably and sanctimoniously, about two Negroes and only two Negroes: Booker T. Washington and George Washington Carver. I left elementary school associating Negro History with the founding of Tuskegee and a scientist who did a great deal with peanuts. I heard something vaguely about Frederick Douglass and something even more vague about Mary McLeod Bethune (who, one of my grade school friends said, after seeing her photograph, looked like a black monkey, for which the teacher, overhearing the remark, promptly slapped him with the yardstick), but I don't recall being taught much of anything about any other Negroes, famous and accomplished or not.

Perhaps how I felt about this as a boy might best be summed up by a particular experience I have never forgotten. In the fifth grade, I was among several students asked to do reports on famous Negroes to present during Negro History Week before the entire school at a special assembly. I was assigned Phillis Wheatley, the noted black colonial poet. We were each "to tell a story about a famous Negro," as our teacher put it. I never did the research for the report. To this day I am not sure why I dawdled, why I did not do the work. I was a conscientious, if not especially brilliant or remarkable, student as a boy. Indeed, it was the absolute assurance the teacher felt that the assignment would be done that landed me the job to begin with. I had no problem doing reports of this sort, and earlier in the year I had completed long reports on Johann Sebastian Bach (when our class did "The Great Composers") and zoology and was quite proud of my work. I felt no greater affinity for either of these projects: I had heard the music of Bach neither before nor during the time I worked on the report and, indeed, was not to hear his music until I reached high school. Zoology, like all sciences, left me indifferent. At the time, my imagination was inflamed by the film *Lawrence of Arabia*, and I would have much preferred doing a report on T. E. Lawrence or the Bedouin than on Bach, zoology, or anything else. I was reading about Lawrence and the Arabs incessantly. Yet, when I went to the library to do the report and found nothing on Wheatley in any encyclopedia, I decided not to search any further or seek the help of the librarian. I simply packed up and went home, puzzled yet benignly at ease with this unaccustomed inertia. I might add that I was not daunted by the prospect of speaking before the school assembly. I had done this on a number of previous occasions, having read the Bible before the school many times. (During my first six years of public schooling, it was not illegal to have Bible reading or class prayer on the premises, nor was it illegal for teachers to practice corporal punishment. Typical of the anxiety of both my age and the era, I was constantly praying not to have an Atomic Bomb dropped on our neighborhood and not to have some bullyboy beat me up!) When Negro History Week finally arrived and our special assembly was called, I was either second or third to give my presentation. There were several white adults in the audience, visitors who came to see us perform, and our white principal was beaming in the light of this demonstration by the school's best and brightest students. Already, knowing I hadn't done the report, I felt a creeping sense of panic within my loins as if at any moment—as I was wont to do when seized by uncontrollable fear and shame—I was going to cry and wet myself. But I also felt a growing sense of defiance and a strangely deepening sense of myself as a person distinct from all the others around me. I realized that I never did the work because I did not want to tell this woman's story or the story of any other Negro.

Those who preceded me were sufficiently parrotlike, reciting with all the indigestible grace of someone who had just swallowed bad medicine after a bad meal. When my time arrived I stood before the audience and said in a very clear, loud voice: "Phillis Wheatley was a famous Negro Poetess." (I thought poetess sounded a bit more learned and correct than poet. I refused to call her a Negress, as black women were referred to in some books I had read. That term seemed insulting to me even then.) "She lived a long time ago," I continued. "She's . . ." I was silent for a long time, having nothing more to say. My teacher, who was particularly depending on my successful performance because I was given one of the more obscure Negroes to report on, seemed visibly concerned with my stumbling. Finally, I concluded, ". . . been dead a long time." I was promptly ushered from the stage amidst a gale of giggles and guffaws. My teacher grabbed me backstage and startled me with a look that seemed a numbingly helpless combination of fury and utter befuddlement.

"Why did you embarrass me and yourself like that? I had been telling the other teachers that your report in particular would be a good one. Why didn't you prepare your report? If you had trouble finding information on her, I would have helped you," she said to me angrily.

"I guess there was some information. I didn't look for any," I said sullenly.

"You what?" she said, genuinely stunned by my acknowledgment that I had not even tried to prepare the report.

For some reason, despite feeling embarrassed and even feeling great pity for my teacher and real guilt about the entire situation, I was glad I hadn't done the report. It occurred to me just at the very moment that I hated Negro History Week, hated it with a vehemence and a contempt that left me speechless and shaking. It seemed to me even then that Negro History Week took "Negro achievements," whatever they were and whatever that meant, and belittled them even more. Everything about it seemed patronizing and inferior. All Negro History Week reminded me of as a boy was that my people had no history worthy of being shared alongside Washington, Jefferson, and the immigrants. It was just a bunch of disembodied names that some other inferiority-afflicted Negro adults told us about so we might know, and be so much the better for knowing, that Negroes had done things in this world. I hated these little stories that were supposed to make us aspire and wish to achieve. What did Phillis Wheatley or Marian Anderson or anybody else mean to me? I looked up at my teacher and wished she would hug me, but she simply stormed away in disgust. I knew I had grown up a little that day, because I did not cry and I did not wet myself.

PRISONER OF RACE

> *. . . from which in my mind I was already free.*
> —ST. AUGUSTINE, *Confessions*, Book IX, Chapter 4

Now, I can hardly shut up during Black History Month. I find myself, noted black professor, on a very modest circuit, speaking before various groups—from black children in run-down schools to upper-middle-class white women at university teas—about the achievements of blacks with, more or less, a sense of performing a necessary and even privileged public service. For one month, after all, this subject—the history of the life and culture of African-Americans—takes on the sainted secularity of a kind of Eve of St. Agnes where we might imagine not an understanding of the past but a utopian future of the races as bridegroom and bride going off to a beatific conjugal bed of neighborly love. Perhaps it is this burdensome yet false weight of history as American civic piety that makes Black History Month, in many respects, such a literally sickening experience for me. After one recent lecture, I went to the rest room immediately and felt the sweat oozing through my clothes, my stomach heaving: Good grief, I thought, how I hate this, how I hate all this besotted and benighted race talk! But why the hell am I doing this?

Woodson dreamed up Negro History Week in order to give black people pride by reminding them of the greatness of their past, a thesis, nay, an obsession that was hardly unique to Woodson and hardly new in Woodson's time. That because of the identity-obliterating force of several hundred years of New World slavery, blacks would be inordinately concerned about both their history, which was denied them by the "master race," and their pride in their peoplehood is not surprising and is quite understandable. Blacks would be a strange people indeed if, under such circumstances, they had any less interest in creating a heroic history than any other group. It was apparent to black people for a long time, even during the age of slavery, that they needed a national identity and a national sense of character—in short, a popular history—and these can only be achieved through convincing people that history is not a tragic burden of sin (as Nathaniel Hawthorne taught us) but a set of simplified myths demonstrating the eschatological meaning of adversity and suffering as millennialism: History was not the fall of Adam but the coming of New Jerusalem. But it is probably the stifling "Parson Weems" stylization of black history that gives it an air of being virtually insufferable and in some real way practically useless, the persistence that, after all, history, in a popular sense, must be heroic and grand if it is to be anything at all. Even during slavery in the nineteenth century, blacks and whites, to create a more redemptive national myth, had already reinvented the Negro: no longer a character without a past, but as Lydia Maria Child, Richard Hildreth, Theodore Parker, William Ellery Channing, William Wells Brown, Ethiop, Forten, Delany, McClune, and others made clear, a character whose grand past presupposed a grander chiliastic and ontological restoration. It is with something like this assumption that Woodson created Negro History Week. This idea of the psychotherapeutic, metaphysical redemption of the Negro has been enlarged to make this week a month and has had bestowed upon it, much to the guilty pleasure of many liberal whites, an intensely Afrocentric and chauvinistic dimension, the seeds of which are also present in what, in truth, is nothing more than a monumental confession that the African-American plays out as a national ritual, a painful drama of psychic exile, identity confusion, double-consciousness that is forced to stand apart from the double-consciousness, the psychic exile, and the identity confusion that afflicts this nation, forcing the African-American's trauma from its central position as *the* double-consciousness of the nation. And even Afrocentricism cannot retrieve what, in fact, no one wishes to have retrieved: the undeniable fact and the undeniable tragedy of slavery, which made us—Africans, black folk, people of color—Americans and westerners at such a terrible, terrible yet deeply profound cost. It is this profundity of utter and absolute exile and shame, heroic because of its absolute defilement and nihilism, to which the Negro can lay claim as being at the heart of Western history and at the heart of American history; and it is this profundity that ultimately is swallowed up in a mediocre vat of anti-intellectual racial, heroic virtue that makes Black History the failure that it is in reimagining African-American national identity and reconfiguring the extent of African-American character or in forcing Americans, black and white, to deal with the true burden of their common history. For in Afrocentrism we have the ultimate tyranny that the black person's history must not simply be asserted as actually having meaning in this world but must be seen as the source, the origin of all meaning in the world. In its search for empires, world domination, genetic superiority, and ultimate psychological wholeness and goodness in all things black, this view does nothing more than ape the unimaginative cultural priorities of the Eurocentrism that it claims to despise but in truth secretly worships in its imitation of its paradigms. This makes the burden of our history, American and Western, beyond the ability of anyone to bear because it does not force us to confront our contradictions but seeks to deny they exist. The real limitation of the creed of Afrocentrism of Pan-Africanism (as with Pan-Germanism or Pan-anything that insists upon the special racial destiny of any people) is that it denies any idea of human transcendence not rooted in race. In short, African-Americans find themselves, by their own invention, trapped in a prison of race that is no more liberating than the prison of race whites constructed for them and that, indeed, offers them no transcendence at all. Like the white Americans who, facing the horror of national "mongrelization" and a cultureless void without history, imagine Europe as the source of the history and the culture to which they aspire, so black Americans, recoiling from the degradation of a brutish and forced "mongrelization" and a cultureless past, look to Africa. Yet the deepest disappointment is black Americans' failure to recognize that they are something remarkably different and, in many respects, remarkably *more* than the African to whom they now genuflect in confused wonder.

Of course, the African-American's Afrocentrism is just another American ethnicity project (despite the vaunted internationalism of its Pan-African implications) that makes history untenable by suggesting that a true historical consciousness is unbearable and offers in its stead a false one that circulates between the poles of a morally aggressive *j'accuse* against the whites (who were colonizers and imperialists, robbers and rapists, after all, by their very nature). This denunciation of whites as morally and genetically inferior, paradoxically, aggrandizes them through the sheer infinitude of the African-Americans' need to have whites' self-evident demonization match their justified outrage, in a kind of 101 appreciation course of "what the Negro has done for modern civilization" that supposedly will make us all better people, as 101 appreciation courses in anything from opera to chemistry are advertised to do. Afrocentrism, in short, has all the worst uplift elements of a typical American moralistic enthusiasm and so, also, does Black History Month.

WHAT I SAW AT THE GATE

> So it was done. You rescued my tongue as you had rescued
> my heart.

—ST. AUGUSTINE, *Confessions*, Book IX, Chapter 4

And what as a boy did I know of history? A few weeks ago, during Black History Month, I was in Philadelphia for a Black Writers' conference. I went down to the old neighborhood in South Philadelphia where I grew up, down around Fifth and Fourth streets and Washington Avenue, Carpenter, Christian, Montrose, Fairhill, and Randolph streets, and I found it older and more shabby, more broken than I could ever remember it having been. The neighborhood, frankly, was filthy: trash-filled empty lots, broken-down homes, the squalid housing projects. "The rock has destroyed this neighborhood," I was told by an acquaintance, meaning the rampant addiction of so many to crack cocaine. One very warm and sunny day, hardly a February day at all, I stood before Sunshine Playground on Christian Street between Fifth and Sixth and remembered how my friends and I played there many years ago when we were children. When I was young, both boys and girls played on the swings and slides, but as I got older, I hung out with the teenage boys who shot baskets and played baseball. The playground was overgrown with weeds as high as small trees and littered with trash of all sorts, broken bottles, cans, little empty plastic vials that were probably crack cocaine containers; the green bars of the gate were rusted shut and padlocked. As I stood there I tried to think of Alex Haley, the grand African-American storyteller and mythmaker who so shrewdly exploited the image of the griot when *Roots*, the book that gave blacks a mythic origin in an Edenic Africa and an immigrant history of overcoming adversity through the story of a great and enduring family, was at the height of its popularity. His sudden death had just been announced a few days earlier, and I had written an op-ed piece on him for the *St. Louis Post-Dispatch*. With both *The Autobiography of Malcolm X*, about a black leader who based his ideology on being both race conscious and theologically non-Western, and *Roots*, one of the grand American stories of race and slavery and the national character, Haley's achievement (despite questions about the authenticity of the authorship) is daunting and probably not as fully appreciated as popular culture events of some magnitude as it ought to be.

But I really was not thinking about Haley at all at that moment. The only person I could think about was an overweight boy with a gimp leg, a few years older than myself, whose name was Poppy and whom we sometimes called the Fatman. He was the best storyteller I ever knew, the best curser I ever knew, the best teller of pornography I ever knew. ("Y'all niggers want to talk about fucking," he once said to us disdainfully during a sex bragging session. "If you ever saw a woman's wet, quivering pussy, you'd run for your lives.") He couldn't play ball like the rest of us, so he was our champion checker player. ("We playing 'touch a man, move a man.' You touch that motherfucker, you gotta move 'im. You ain't no jury, so don't be doin' no deliberatin'," he told me once when I sat down to play him. He then proceeded to beat me in a blizzard of moves that positively blinded me. "Next chump?" he called after I was humiliated.) The Fatman was also our resident rhetorician and storyteller, telling long, elaborate jokes about the black man, white man, and China man, politically incorrect ethnic stories that made all of us boys laugh uproariously. Sometimes in the jokes, tales really, the black man would be the goat and at other times he would be the hero, but the jokes were equally funny either way. Sometimes, they were virtually lessons.

"Once upon a time, there was a white man, China man, and a black man and they each get a thousand dollars. The white man say, 'I'm gonna invest this money on Wall Street in stocks and shit,' and off he go to invest his money. The China man, he say, 'I'm gonna get my relatives and open me a Chinese restaurant in a nigger neighborhood 'cause I know them niggers love Chinese food and I'm gonna make me some money.' The black man take that money, look at it real close to make sure it's real. Then he say, 'I'm getting me some Ripple wine, some women, and I'm gonna lay back and enjoy myself on this here fine day.' Who do you think did the best thing with the money?"

We would argue this back and forth. Some of the boys would say the white man did the smartest thing by investing the money on Wall Street. "That's how white people get rich," one of us would say. Some would think the China man was the smartest for starting a restaurant and running his own business. "That's what black people need to do: start they own business in the neighborhood," one of us would say. No one picked the black man as the smartest.

"I didn't ask you nigger who did the smartest thing with the money," the Fatman said. "I asked who did the best thing with the money. And the answer is the black man."

"Aw, man, that's a lot of bullshit. That's what white people want us to do with money. Go around and spend it and have a good time," someone would answer disgustedly.

"What the white man gonna do with that money but go gamble. And why he wanna gamble? To make more money so he can do what the black man wanna do: have a good time. What the China man wanna do? Make more money by selling shit so he can have a good time. That black wanna do the best thing 'cause he wanna have a good time and he don't want to have it at somebody else's expense. He don't want to be making more money off people being greedy and shit when he can have a good time with what he got. Besides, the white man invest in Wall Street and lose all his money; the China man's restaurant gets burned down. So, what them motherfuckers got to show for the money. Nothing! So, the black man doing the best thing with the money but not the smartest thing." As a boy, I think these jokes, these stories which the Fatman told us, were the real and only black history for which I felt anything, the only American history that meant something to me, that reverberated in my being as something profound, wise, inspirited, crafted, joyous, yet tragic. Those boys, that playground, those stories, were the only real racial solidarity I have ever known, the only real racial consciousness I have ever felt. Standing at the gate I did not long for its return but only for an understanding of what it was and what it meant. Perhaps, as I entered my middle age as a black man in America, the Fatman, at that moment, may have been able to help me understand what I felt and what I was destined to feel. "Sometimes you ain't a fool but most of the time you are, sometimes you dream lucky, but most of the time you don't, what the hell else is there to say? That's life in America and every fucking place else," he was fond of telling us boys. As I stood by the gates of Sunshine Center, I suddenly missed the Fatman a great deal, missed those stories more than I thought possible. The Fatman died more than a dozen years ago from acute alcoholism, but when I last saw him, thin, sick, and very drunk, when I was a graduate student at Cornell visiting Philadelphia one summer, he told me, "Happy [one of my nicknames because I always looked so serious and sad], I'm glad you made it off the block." Off one block and onto another. That's what I wanted to tell him, in the end. There's always a block one is trying to get off of. And for any black person in America the word "block" resonates historically and culturally: Is it true, finally and at last, that there is, in the words of that old black spiritual, no more auction block for me?

As I sit in front of my home in an all-white, affluent neighborhood with my golden retriever, with my children who speak in the white patois using such terms as "rad," "gross," and "super," with my wife who drives a Chevy van, the car of the white housewife as it is called, although my wife is neither; as I sit and look across the street at a house for sale and the people, all white and all presumably middle class, who go through examining it on an unseasonably warm early March afternoon, I notice that some wave at me, some are indeed quite happy to know me, some ignore me, a smaller number look at me oddly as if to say, "Oh, blacks live here, too." I sometimes think that the wide expanse of Sunshine Center is no whit wider than the sides of this street on which I live. As I sit here I would like to ask my friend, the Fatman, did I do the smartest thing or the best thing?

susan straight

susan straight

Susan Straight was born in 1960 in Riverside, California, and still lives in the neighborhood in which she grew up. She attended the local public schools, where she met her husband when she was fourteen. Straight received her M.F.A. in Creative Writing from the University of Massachusetts, Amherst, where she studied with Jay Neugeboren, James Baldwin, and Julius Lester. She teaches now at the University of California, Riverside.

Straight has published short stories in *TriQuarterly, The North American Review, Ploughshares*, the *Los Angeles Times Magazine*, and *The Pushcart Prize XVI*. She is the author of four published novels: *Aquaboogie: A Novel in Stories, I've Been in Sorrow's Kitchen and Licked Out All the Pots, Blacker Than a Thousand Midnights,* and *The Gettin Place.*

The characters in Susan Straight's fiction reflect the mixed-race neighborhood in which she has spent most of her life. "At readings," she says, "there's always somebody who's surprised to see that I'm white. 'Sorry,' I tell them, 'this is me, and this is the way I naturally talk.' "

my two mothers

My mother-in-law's face, when she had been in a coma for two weeks, was sculpted and elegant, with planed cheekbones and the moles near her eyes starkly defined. Her skin was the palest gold, like unripe apricots, instead of the rich reddish-brown I had known for twenty years. Because all of us women attending her, her daughters-in-law and foster daughter and neighbors and friends, had been unable to color and straighten her hair, it was fading to silver around her forehead, and the strands were drawn up in a tight bun. "She looks like a model," her foster daughter whispered to me one night. "But she don't look like Alberta."

She didn't. Her feet were what we worried about. My mother-in-law had been admitted to the county general hospital for vision problems, had been told she had an infected artery near her eye, but after three days she was much worse. The invisible and insidious combination of high blood pressure and stress, fear and intravenous steroids began to send small strokes through the back of her brain. She would turn incoherent and sightless, then seem to recover. After being moved to intensive care, where one of us spent the night in the waiting room and beside her bed, she kept asking me to translate her condition for her. Since I'd had sick children in the past, and I wasn't afraid to talk to the doctors or ask questions, I was the family spokesperson. When I told her what was happening, all Alberta would ask was, "Don't tell General."

She didn't want her husband of forty years to worry. She wanted to know how he was taking it, who was feeding him, whether he was drinking. We, the other women and me, rubbed her feet. She was uncomfortable, being cared for like that.

She slipped into a coma early in the morning, while I was downstairs looking for a soda for my three-year-old, and her feet began to fall to the sides almost immediately. "Don't let her feet drop like that!" my sister-in-law said. As a nurse's aide in a convalescent home, she knew what those hopeless splayed feet meant.

And Alberta loved shoes. She had large feet, size ten, and expensive taste in shoes. They filled her closet, crowded boxes under her bed and in cupboards. She suffered corns and bunions for narrow-toed elegance and high heels. She bore seven children, raised six of them and countless nieces and nephews and children in need; she fed twenty or thirty people in a day, men who worked with her husband or sons, neighbors who could always fill a dinner plate at her stove, even casual acquaintances who always seemed to stop by around dinnertime to hear, "Go get you somethin' in the kitchen."

For two weeks I massaged her feet, with their rough gray spots and pale heels, propping them on pillows, moving them. The other women and I turned her in the bed, checked her tubes, and talked to her. I hadn't told anyone except my husband that I was pregnant with our third child. He whispered it into her ear a few hours after she went into the coma; all of us women talked to her constantly. Her face paled and turned childlike, smooth; we took off her wedding ring.

I've been married to her son for twelve years, but I've been with him for twenty. I've outlasted all the other daughters-in-law, the women from her three other sons. When the social workers and others needed to fill out papers, I was the only one who knew all her important dates, the jobs she'd had, all the stories she'd told me over these many years while she sat in her big chair by the fireplace and I sat shelling pecans or nursing a baby.

Every day that month of her illness, I took my kids and my neighbor's to school, I went to work, and I came straight to the hospital. Before she stopped talking, Alberta wouldn't tell me how she felt, how her head or eyes or chest hurt. Instead, she asked me how the girls were, what I'd fed them for dinner, whether my husband was tired. Everyone was more important than she was. That was one of the things she'd taught me, all those years. And I stayed with her until visiting time was over; then I went home to cook and clean and do laundry. That was what my mother had taught me, too.

My first memory is a dim day in a dusty room, with a wooden Swiss clock ticking hollow and my mother crying. She couldn't hold me on her lap because she didn't have one. She was eight months pregnant. I was three. My father was gone. He didn't come back.

From what my mother tells me, she cried for two days, and then she went back to work. I went to a series of baby-sitters, as always. We ate oatmeal. I was opinionated. One day I refused to eat my oatmeal. My mother slapped me so hard the spoon hit the wall. According to her, I said, "You can hit me, but I'm still not eating it." That was the only time she lost her temper.

She had my little brother soon after. Her stepmother said, on the phone, "You made your bed, you must lie in it." She brought him home, where he threw up all over the yellow bassinet. A huge dust storm had filled the tiny one-bedroom house with fine silt. She cried again. Then she went to work, the next day, where she'd worked for several years: Household Finance, where she was supposed to be the secretary but was really managing the franchise for an alcoholic supervisor. My father had met her when he came in for a loan.

She ran the office, picked us up, cleaned and cooked and did laundry. She wrote a letter to the main office in Chicago, explaining that she deserved to be the manager since she was doing managerial work. She received a return letter stating that it would be a cold day in hell before a woman would be a manager at Household Finance. I think the irony of the company's title makes my mother's double life in those days even more poignant; she taught me that only hard work, more work, harder work, would get me anywhere, but it didn't succeed in the early 1960s.

My mother never told me stories when I was young. She showed me how to wash dishes properly, how to wash clothes, how to scrub floors on my knees and scrub walls with ammonia. I was the oldest girl. I started doing housework when I was seven. We cleaned together. She didn't tell me awful stories about my natural father, or tales about her life in Switzerland, where she was born. She married again, a man who worked in her office, had another boy right away, and cared for foster children for ten years.

I can clean anything. We cleaned rental houses, my stepfather's vacated apartments, his laundries. He took good care of us, and we took care of rooms and meals and residences. When I clean my house now, I do it exactly the way my mother taught me. Often I am on my knees.

But she was determined that I would go to college. When no counselors at my high school were interested in helping with applications, she and I did them. She was never effusive. Never demonstrative. Not huggy or kissy. She wanted me to work harder.

My mother's mother died when she was ten. She sat in the front room with her mother's body for two days, in the Swiss town where she lived. Her father married the nurse who'd lived with them during her mother's illness. So my mother grew up with the consummate evil stepmother, who didn't love her, didn't even pretend to like her. When the family emigrated to frozen winter in Canada, her stepmother tried to marry her off to a pig farmer. She was seventeen. She went to live elsewhere, with a Canadian family. Eventually, when her parents moved to southern California, my mother came, too, but she never slept in their house. She moved to a rooming house here, in Riverside, and began working in the office where she met my father.

She didn't tell me the truth about him, or much of anything about her family, until the day I graduated from college. She told me how my father left, not the dusty clock and room part, but the part where he met another woman. He was a salesman. The kind of man who eventually leaves everyone, I gathered. He had children I didn't know. He had three wives.

And the essence of her story, one of the first stories she'd ever told, was that men leave. And only hard work saves a woman.

• • •

I waited until Dwayne and I had been married seven years before I had kids. We'd met in eighth grade, married when I was twenty-two. My mother told me, the day before, "When you get married, you give away fifty percent of your life." That was it, the big preparation for my romantic future. My husband's aunts took me aside and lectured me on cooking properly for a black man; they had a few drinks and told me straight up they weren't sure how they felt about the first white person to marry into the family.

But Dwayne's mother, Alberta, said she was so glad we were in love. She never said anything mean to me in my life. She had ways of expressing her displeasure, but they were soft, smiling, and roundabout. Hard work, housework, were just as important to her. She taught me to cook things my mother didn't make, how to use lemon pepper and garlic salt on chicken, neckbones or hamhocks in beans, how to soften up a cheap, tough roundsteak.

They both taught me that a woman has to work to keep a man. He has only to exist. Fortunately, Dwayne had learned to take rudimentary care of himself, his food and clothing, when he was in college. Unfortunately, I kept waiting for him to leave.

They'd all left, my girlfriends' husbands, my girlfriends' fathers, my father. I waited. Dwayne waited for me to figure out he wasn't going anywhere. Alberta waited for our children. "You can't be a woman till you have kids," she said. When I got pregnant, my mother told me in that same voice, "Now you're giving away the other fifty percent."

I do all the things I was taught to do. I work all the time. I work three jobs. I've had three jobs since I was fifteen, cleaning houses and working in a theater and helping my mother. Now I teach in a university, I clean and cook and wash, I spend every waking moment I'm not working with my daughters, and when they go to bed, I hang up one more load of wash before I sit down at the typewriter to work a few more hours. From six-thirty to past midnight, I do what I was taught women should do and what I figured out I should do. It takes longer than one eight-hour shift. They were both right, Alberta and my mother. For me, my children are my life. Just as Alberta always put them before me, so do I. I gave away all the rest of it. My mother stops by, mentions my less-than-spotless floor, sometimes shakes her head and often offers to help. On her knees. While I'm on mine.

What do I pass on to my girls? Hard work. They see that. But they see me write, too. They see Dwayne cook, even if it's only now and then and only macaroni and cheese. They see him iron his own clothes, which shocks and outrages his father.

Nine years ago, Dwayne (who *likes* to iron while watching television, OK?) was standing over the slanted board in our tiny apartment. He asked if he could press something for me, so I handed him the black skirt I was preparing to wear for work that day. His father walked in while he was ironing it, and I still hear the tale at least twice a year. "And she makes the boy iron her clothes!" he shouts, disbelieving.

Alberta did everything. And in the hospital, she told my sister-in-law, "I'm so tired. I don't think I want to go home just yet."

She was only sixty-one. She had retired, but taking care of all those people every day was harder than the office work she'd done for ten years after her kids were grown. For several months she'd been suffering from severe headaches—I found out when she began slipping away; she'd been lying down in the middle of the day, when no one was around. But she didn't want to tell anyone. She didn't want to bother or worry them.

The last week of her life, we moved her to a hospice on the advice of the doctors, who said her brain could not recover. Her body was shutting down. The hospice was a few blocks from our house. We went every night, Dwayne and me and the girls; the women and I lasted much longer by her bedside than the men, even her sons. We talked to her, put lotion on her skin, worried about her hair and her grown-out fingernails showing crescents of unpolished pink lightening to bloodless white. If she had been able to talk, she would have only asked what everyone was eating at her house, who was taking care of her kitchen. She couldn't talk. She breathed shallow, then labored. We put balm on her dry lips.

When my mother finally came to see Alberta, she cried uncontrollably and then grew angry with me. Why wasn't I crying? Because I'd been doing this for a month already. It didn't shock me anymore. Why wasn't I taking better care of her? I bit my lips and watched my mother, the exact antithesis of my mother-in-law. My mother, who is sixty, is under five feet, tiny and quick, blue-eyed and sharp-featured, and never cosmetically changed. Alberta was lying in bed. But standing, living, she was five-nine, large-boned, and soft-faced, always made up. She moved slowly, gracefully.

My mother was angry with me until the last night. She had just retired herself, had just begun telling me stories about her mother this year. I don't think she'd ever gotten over losing the only person who truly loved her. She and Alberta taught me about sacrifice, and they had to be right.

My husband had just left Alberta's bedside at ten that night, and during the few minutes as he left the parking lot for home, she died. When he pulled into the driveway, I had already gotten the call from his foster sister. I was getting ready to go myself. He went to get his father, I left the girls with my neighbor, and I went to be with the women.

Five of us sat with her body for a long time, crying, touching her, trying to close her mouth, lamenting her hair and hands and her limp, graceless feet. Her three other sons couldn't stay in the room; her husband couldn't bring himself to come, Dwayne said. We stayed until we were ready to leave.

In the parking lot, though, I broke down. I told Revia and Shirley and the others, all of us thirty or forty, with jobs and kids and too much work and now no Alberta, that all I could see ahead of me was loss. We were at that age now, losing parents, tending sick children, too tired for our own selves to smile half the time.

It took a long time for them to talk me out of that. "You got another baby coming," they said. I didn't want it to be a sad baby. "It's your job to make it a happy baby," Alberta used to say.

The night after her funeral, I cleaned Alberta's kitchen furiously and thoroughly. On my knees. My mother couldn't come to the service; she came to see Alberta's face at the viewing the night before, and she cried bitterly, much harder than I did, in public. They were good friends who traded fried chicken and homemade jam and their grandchildren. I listened to my mother's sobs, heard her say, "Now she looks like herself. They took good care of her."

The neighbor women had done her hair and makeup. She was Alberta again. Even though the funeral director said she shouldn't have shoes, Dwayne insisted she wear silver-sequined low heels.

We fed over a hundred people in her tiny front room, in the driveway and street and the kitchen. I kept chasing them out after a few hours. I washed the dishes and cleaned out the entire refrigerator and wiped down the stove and counters. Then I scrubbed the floor, and I hollered at anyone who tried to come onto the linoleum until Dwayne came to take me out to the car. I was three months pregnant. I shouldn't be working that hard, people kept saying. But for a few minutes, at least, I stared at the gleaming surfaces and felt like I knew what I was doing.

Alberta's sister-in-law, her husband's oldest sister, died within the month. We had another funeral. And, though this is the hardest thing I've ever written, it taught me something: The morning of that service, my father-in-law was distraught, saying that he'd never missed Alberta as much as then because there was no one to help him prepare food for guests and clean the house. I was meant to do it, along with my sisters-in-law. The work wouldn't have bothered me. It was the words.

I was angrier than I've been in a long time, though I said nothing. And I know my father-in-law loved his wife immensely, had for many years. But in the car, I told Dwayne that when I died, if I heard him say he missed me for my cooking or my ability to bleach his socks, I would come back from wherever I was and make his life a living hell. "You can miss my smile or my voice or lots of other parts," I told him. "But you better not miss my cooking or cleaning. No."

They taught me well, my mother and Alberta. My mother's still working on me. I finished my next book, months after the funerals, and when my mother stopped by and I told her, she nodded and said, "Your yard's a mess and that tree needs trimming." I'm seven months pregnant. I don't think Dwayne's leaving. But there's so much work to be done. And I can't do it without some love.

Alberta's kitchen was clean, I was having scary pains, the girls were apprehensive in the back seat, and Dwayne took me home. He lay me in the bed while I finally cried and cried, and he brought me something to eat. Then he washed the dishes.

henry louis gates, jr.

henry louis gates, jr.

Henry Louis Gates, Jr., was born in 1950 in West Virginia. In his application to Yale in 1969, he began his personal statement, "My grandfather was colored, my father was a Negro, and I am black." After graduating from Yale, Gates became the first black American to earn a Ph.D. in English from Cambridge University, where he studied with Nobel laureate Wole Soyinka.

His works include *Signifying Monkey: A Theory of Afro-American Literary Criticism*, which won the American Book Award, *Colored People: A Memoir*, and *The Classic Slave Narratives*, a collection of lost texts by African-Americans that Gates unearthed, prompting Maya Angelou to call him "a wonderful mixture of Alex Haley and Sherlock Holmes."

The recipient of a MacArthur Award in 1980, Henry Louis Gates, Jr., is now W.E.B. Du Bois Professor of the Humanities and chairman of the Afro-American Studies Department at Harvard. Arguably America's most visible public intellectual, Gates writes stylish and insightful essays for *The New Yorker*, in which all manner of public figures open their souls to him.

letter to my daughters

Dear Maggie and Liza:

I have written to you because a world into which I was born, a world that nurtured and sustained me, has mysteriously disappeared. My darkest fear is that Piedmont, West Virginia, will cease to exist if some executives on Park Avenue decide that it is more profitable to build a completely new paper mill elsewhere than to overhaul one a century old. Then they would close it, just as they did in Cumberland with Celanese, and Pittsburgh Plate Glass, and the Kelly-Springfield Tire Company. The town will die, but our people will not move. They will not *be* moved. Because for them, Piedmont—snuggled between the Allegheny Mountains and the Potomac River valley—is life itself.

I have written to you because of the day when we were driving home and you asked your mother and me just exactly what the civil rights movement had been all about and I pointed to a motel on Route 2 and said that at one time I could not have stayed there. Your mother could have stayed there, but your mother couldn't have stayed there with me. And you kids looked at us like we were telling you the biggest lie you had ever heard. So I thought about writing to you.

I have written for another reason, as well. I remember that once we were walking in Washington, D.C., heading for the National Zoo, and you asked me if I had known the man to whom I had just spoken. I said no. And, Liza, you volunteered that you found it embarrassing that I would speak to a complete stranger on the street. It called to mind a trip I'd made to Pittsburgh with my father. On the way from his friend Mr. Ozzie Washington's sister's house, I heard Daddy speak to a colored man, then saw him tip his hat to the man's wife. (Daddy liked nice hats: Caterpillar hats for work, Dobbs hats for Sunday.) It's just something that you do, he said, when I asked him if he had known those people and why had he spoken to them.

Last summer, I sat at a sidewalk cafe in Italy, and three or four "black" Italians walked casually by, as well as a dozen or more blacker Africans. Each spoke to me; rather, each nodded his head slightly or acknowledged me by a glance, ever so subtly. When I was growing up, we always did this with each other, passing boats in a sea of white folk.

Yet there were certain Negroes who would avoid acknowledging you in this way in an integrated setting, especially if the two of you were the ones doing the integrating. Don't go over there with those white people if all you're going to do is Jim Crow yourselves—Daddy must have said that to me a thousand times. And by that I think he meant we shouldn't *cling* to each other out of habit or fear, or use protective coloration to evade the risks of living like any other human being, or use clannishness as a cop-out for exploring ourselves and possibly making new selves, forged in the crucible of integration. Your black ass, he'd laugh, is integrated already.

But there are other reasons that people distrust the reflex—the nod, the glance, the murmured greeting.

One reason is a resentment at being lumped together with thirty million African-Americans whom you don't know and most of whom you will never know. Completely by the accident of racism, we have been bound together with people with whom we may or may not have something in common, just because we are "black." Thirty million Americans are black, and thirty million is a lot of people. One day you wonder: What do the misdeeds of a Mike Tyson have to do with me? So why do I feel implicated? And how can I not feel racial recrimination when I can feel racial pride?

Then, too, there were Negroes who were embarrassed about *being* Negroes, who didn't want to be bothered with race and with other black people. One of the more painful things about being colored was being colored in public around other colored people, who were embarrassed to be colored and embarrassed that we *both* were colored and in public together. As if to say: "Negro, will you *pul-lease* disappear so that I can get my own white people?" As if to say: "I'm not a Negro like other Negroes." As if to say: "I am a human being—let me be!"

For much of my adolescence and adulthood, I thought of these people as having betrayed the race. I used to walk up to them and call them *Brother* or *Sister*, loud and with a sardonic edge, when they looked like they were trying to "escape." When I went off to college, I would make the "conversion" of errant classmates a serious project, a political commitment.

I used to reserve my special scorn for those Negroes who were always being embarrassed by someone else in the race. Someone too dark, someone too "loud," someone too "wrong," someone who dared to wear red in public. Loud and wrong—we used to say that about each other. Nigger is loud and wrong. "Loud" carried a triple meaning: speaking too loudly, dressing too loudly, and just *being* too loudly.

I do know that, when I was a boy, many Negroes would have been the first to censure other Negroes once they were admitted into all-white neighborhoods or schools or clubs. "An embarrassment to the race"—phrases of that sort were bandied about. Accordingly, many of us in our generation engaged in strange antics to flout those strictures. Like eating watermelon in public, eating it loudly and merrily, and spitting the seeds into the middle of the street, red juice running down the sides of our cheeks, collecting under our chins. Or taking the greatest pride in the Royal Kink. Uncle Harry used to say he didn't *like* watermelon, which I knew was a lie because I saw him wolf down slices when I was a little kid, before he went off to seminary at Boston University. But he came around, just like he came around to painting God and Jesus black, and all the seraphim and the cherubim, too. And I, from another direction, have gradually come around also, and stopped trying to tell other Negroes how to be black.

Do you remember when your mother and I woke you up early on a Sunday morning, just to watch Nelson Mandela walk out of prison, and how it took a couple of hours for him to emerge, and how you both wanted to go back to bed and, then, to watch cartoons? And how we began to worry that something bad had happened to him on the way out, because the delay was so long? And when he finally walked out of that prison, how we were so excited and teary-eyed at Mandela's nobility, his princeliness, his straight back and unbowed head? I think I felt that there walked the Negro, as Pop might have said; there walked the whole of the African people, as regal as any king. And that feeling I had, that gooseflesh sense of identity that I felt at seeing Nelson Mandela, listening to Mahalia Jackson sing, watching Muhammad Ali fight, or hearing Martin Luther King speak, is part of what I mean by being colored. I realize the sentiment may not be logical, but I want to have my cake and eat it, too. Which is why I still nod or speak to black people on the streets and why it felt so good to be acknowledged by the Afro-Italians who passed my table at the cafe in Milan.

I want to be able to take special pride in a Jessye Norman aria, a Muhammad Ali shuffle, a Michael Jordan slam dunk, a Spike Lee movie, a Thurgood Marshall opinion, a Toni Morrison novel, James Brown's Camel Walk. Above all, I enjoy the unselfconscious moments of a shared cultural intimacy, whatever form they take, when no one else is watching, when no white people are around. Like Joe Louis's fights, which my father still talks about as part of the fixed repertoire of stories that texture our lives. You've seen his eyes shining as he describes how Louis hit Max Schmeling so many times and so hard, and how some reporter asked him, after the fight: "Joe, what would you have done if that last punch hadn't knocked Schmeling out?" And how ole Joe responded, without missing a beat: "I'da run around behind him to see what was holdin' him up!"

Even so, I rebel at the notion that I can't be part of other groups, that I can't construct identities through elective affinity, that race must be the most important thing about me. Is that what I want on my gravestone: Here lies an African-American? So I am divided. I want to be black, to know black, to luxuriate in whatever I might be calling blackness at any particular time—but to do so in order to come out the other side, to experience a humanity that is neither colorless nor reducible to color. Bach *and* James Brown. Sushi *and* fried catfish. Part of me admires those people who can say with a straight face that they have transcended any attachment to a particular community or group . . . but I always want to run around behind them to see what holds them up.

I am not Everynegro. I am not native to the great black metropolises: New York, Chicago, or Los Angeles, say. Nor can I claim to be a "citizen of the world." I am from and of a time and a place—Piedmont, West Virginia—and that's a world apart, a world of difference. So this is not a story of a race but a story of a village, a family, and its friends. And of a sort of segregated peace. What hurt me most about the glorious black awakening of the late sixties and early seventies is that we lost our sense of humor. Many of us thought that enlightened politics excluded it.

In your lifetimes, I suspect, you will go from being African-Americans, to "people of color," to being, once again, "colored people." (The linguistic trend toward condensation is strong.) I don't mind any of the names myself. But I have to confess that I like "colored" best, maybe because when I hear the word, I hear it in my mother's voice and in the sepia tones of my childhood. As artlessly and honestly as I can, I have tried to evoke a colored world of the fifties, a Negro world of the early sixties, and the advent of a black world of the later sixties, from the point of view of the boy I was. When you are old enough to read what follows, I hope that it brings you even a small measure of understanding, at long last, of why we see the world with such different eyes . . . and why that is for me a source both of gladness and of regret. And I hope you'll understand why I continue to speak to colored people I pass on the streets.

Love,
Daddy

Piedmont, West Virginia
July 8, 1993

naomi shihab nye

naomi shihab nye

Naomi Shihab Nye was born in 1952 to a Palestinian father and an American mother. She grew up in St. Louis, and as a teenager lived in Jerusalem and Ramallah, Jordan. She finished high school in San Antonio, Texas, where she now lives with her husband and son.

Her books of poetry are: *Different Ways to Pray, Hugging the Jukebox*, selected for the National Poetry Series, *Yellow Glove, Red Suitcase*, and *Words Under Words*. Nye is also the author and editor of a number of award-winning children's books, including *Sitti's Secret, Benito's Dream Bottle*, and *This Same Sky*.

The late poet William Stafford called Nye "a champion of the literature of encouragement and heart." Nye is reminiscent of poets from other countries in which writers more commonly double as ambassadors or peacemakers. She is a popular guest at both national and international conferences and workshops. In San Antonio, where she claims to have taught writing to every child going through the schools in the last twenty years, she rises each dawn to the insistent first-person appeal of the rooster penned in her backyard.

widening the circle

Once, in a grocery store in St. Louis in the 1950s, my mother stared hard at a regal black woman checking out next to us and whispered to me, "I feel closer to her than to my own people." I thought about this for a long time. My mother's favorite singers, whom we played again and again on the phonograph, were Mahalia Jackson, Marian Anderson, and Harry Belafonte. I knew she had rejected at least the religious elements of her own heritage—strict German Missouri Synod Lutheran—which was partly what attracted her to my Palestinian immigrant, nonpracticing Muslim father. He was as different from "her own people" as she could get—unless, perhaps, she had married someone black. That would have been more difficult, she said.

It was hard for me to understand where the lines were drawn, and why.

There were no black students in my school. Our neighborhood, Ferguson, sidled up to Kinloch, a black neighborhood we sometimes drove through. It felt like a different world over there, poorer, but more animated. I had heard that some fanatical residents on our side wanted to build a fence between the two sectors. Luckily I never met them. Our own neighborhood contained Italian-American, French-Canadian, and "regular" white American families, whatever that meant, but no other Palestinians, for sure. When people said it was very brave for my father to run for PTA president (he won) and later for the school board (he lost), I didn't get it. What made it braver for him than for anyone else? In those days I would no sooner have called myself an Arab-American than a girl from the moon, though I knew I was half-and-half, like thick milk, and shuddered a little whenever a "halfbreed" showed up in any of the weird Wild West tales we still read in school.

I didn't know any black Americans personally until I took my first brief summer job at age twelve, picking berries on a local farm. I was the only semi-white picker, and the only girl.

The boys I stooped with over the strawberry rows lived in Kinloch, and I asked them lots of questions: What was their school like? Did they go downtown to the riverfront very much? Did they like to ride the bus? For me, city buses were a high point of St. Louis integration. The boys seemed to find me humorous, so naturally I talked overtime. I told them my father was an Arab, and then they had some questions to ask *me*. Did we have a tent? Did we eat camel soup? I was not in-sulted. Our differences felt enlivening, not threatening. I wished the berry season lasted longer.

In St. Louis in those days, people talked disparagingly about neigh-borhoods that were "going." My mother's father dragged his dirty clothes to the Laundromat in a wheeled cart at three in the morning so he could be assured of being there by himself. His neighborhood was "going" black—but I didn't get it. Were black neighborhoods—being "gone"—no longer there? What made some "others" like my father easily accepted and other "others" not? Occasionally I caught a late-night tale sliding under the crack of our bedroom door—some-one had been mean to my father because of "who he was"—but by morning this rumor would have disappeared. Our father was resilient, and if someone was mean, well, he would just be nicer.

Our home swirled with immigrants passing through, Greeks and Lebanese—my father attracted them like a magnet. Sometimes the living room would be filled with Arabic, which my brother and I were not learning, and our friends' ears would prickle curiously. Who were we, after all? I felt slightly mysterious, even to myself. I was always standing with one foot held back out of the circle. Because I did not quite "fit in," I thought I could make a clean getaway at any moment. It was a power source, not a liability. My brother had much darker skin than I did. No one ever mentioned *my* skin. We had a family, a world, and a faraway culture I would not see until 1966 when, at the age of fourteen, we moved to what was then the Jordanian side of Jerusalem.

Like thousands of others, my Palestinian relatives had lost their home and money in the bank to Zionists when the state of Israel was formed in 1948. They gazed longingly across the no-man's-land toward the old stone house they could no longer see. Now they lived in a small, simple village. We rented a flat near a refugee camp and took walks along its perimeters. The dispirited alienation of families that had lost everything except their own lives rose up from that place like a gloomy cloud. The Palestinians were, to the Jews, what the black population was to white St. Louis—second-class citizens, unfortunate realities, undeserving "others." How did these things happen? Shouldn't the Jews have been more sensitive than anyone else about such disparity? At night, from our house, we could hear guns firing in Israel, soldiers practicing their aim.

I was most fascinated by tales that Zionists liked to say "Palestinians" had never existed. Didn't they have eyes and ears? Zionists pretended "Israel"—a word Palestinians had trouble even saying back then—had sprung into existence in a barren, uninhabited land. Zionists had feelings only for their own honor. The concept of a chosen people—no matter if Jew or Nazi, lighter or darker, or any style of orthodox—bore a hideous gleam to me. This was how wars began. This was the heart of all evil.

I attended school with Armenians, another group of alienated refugees entirely, in the ancient Armenian convent sector of the Old City. The massacres of their own ancestors by the Turkish armies eclipsed the local troubles in their eyes. Their crowded homes, stacked like beehives, bore photographs of their lost world. I was the only non-Armenian student enrolled; the faculty was not thrilled about my presence. But the students seemed happy to have someone show up "from the outside." People seemed to get exhausted by "their own kind" if they didn't know anyone else. That's what my classmates said. "We're sick of ourselves. So tell us a new story, *okay*?" I still keep that little folded-up note. By now I prized "being different" as if it were a lucky medal.

After the Six-Day War in 1967 (we flew back to the United States immediately prior to its start, leaving our car in the driveway and our beds made), during which the now-famous West Bank territories were occupied by Israelis, the suffering of my father's people dramatically increased. Living in a village under occupation, they were subjected to prison terms, continual harassment, bullets and tear gas, seizure of their vineyards and olive groves for "settlements" by outsiders, and inflated taxation. On later trips back, my father finally got to see his stolen home again—it was now occupied by rabbinical students from Brooklyn. Occupied Palestinians had no civil rights whatsoever—all these things have recently become more widely known. My father used to ask Americans who knew little about Palestine how they would feel if an American Indian appeared on their doorstep and said, Sorry, this was my home first, my gods promised it to me. Would they be willing to move out and give it all up?

Each time I returned to the West Bank as an adult, I had experiences that made me grit my teeth and swear—guns pointed in my face, rough interrogations, witnessing vicious attacks on Arab citizens, tear gas, and despicable rudeness on the part of those with weapons. I could easily have picked up the biggest stones available to pitch at soldiers along with rowdy Intifada boys. I hated my own country for giving Israelis the guns. It was confusing. Now I knew what segregation felt like and how enormous the flare of anger could be in response. It amazed me that there wasn't *more* violence among oppressed people everywhere. How long could they stand it? In the West Bank, even little things would set me off—seeing the Hebrew language printed so much larger than the Arabic language on signs, for example. When asked about politics, my grandmother, who lived to be 106 and died right before the "semi-autonomy" of Gaza and Jericho took effect, would tip her whimsical head and say, "I never lost my peace *inside*."

Luckily, I met many Jews over the years, both in the United States and Israel, who had a deeper concept of what the Jewish-Arab relationship could and should have been—cousins, from the start, and mutual supporters, yes? Why not? What did exclusivity ever have to offer but a distorted, unrealistic view of the world? People who stuck only to their own kind were scared people. I could apply that to my memories of St. Louis, too.

One of the Jewish women who founded Women in Black, the group that gathered to protest unfair occupation tactics and cruel treatment of Arabs for years, came to see me with a huge bruise on her cheek. I felt terrible to learn it had come from a pitched stone as she drove by a refugee camp. To hit her, of all people! She shrugged. "People who speak out for others' rights always take risks. But there are encouraging moments—one day a bus pulled up to our group of demonstrators, filled with Palestinian women in their beautiful em-broidered dresses and white scarves. They didn't get out but pressed their faces to the windows. Their eyes met ours—no word was ex-changed. But we knew then that *they knew* what we had been doing for them. It was enough fuel to keep us going for as long as we had to." I knew at that moment that the real heroes of race and culture would always be the people who stepped out of their own line to make a larger circle.

jessica hagedorn

jessica hagedorn

Jessica Hagedorn was born in the Philippines in 1949. She immigrated to the United States when she was fourteen and spent her adolescence in San Francisco, where she studied theater arts at the American Conservatory Theater. She began publishing her poetry widely in the late sixties and has worked as a performance artist.

Her books of poetry and prose include *Dangerous Music* and *Pet Food and Tropical Apparitions*. Her much celebrated novel *Dogeaters* received a Beyond Columbus award and was nominated for a National Book Award. She is the editor of *Charlie Chan Is Dead: An Anthology of Contemporary Asian American Fiction*.

Jessica Hagedorn's writing, in poetry and prose, is lush, cinematic, and wildly musical. She lives in New York City, where she has been, for many years, the leader and lyricist of the Ganster Choir Band.

the exile within/
the question of identity

There are questions that come to mind when exploring or attempting to define "Asian American culture" and my own influences as a writer and artist. Should the question actually be "What is American culture?" And is the solution inevitably, "Multiculturalism"?

"Your universe is shrinking!" The white man in Salman Rushdie's controversial novel, *The Satanic Verses*, warns the actor Saladin Chamcha (one of the novel's main characters) before Chamcha turns into a goat-like devil. Rushdie's white man is a successful TV producer, and the universe he is referring to is a racial universe. "Aliens," as the quintessential white man calls people of color, are no longer in. Aliens aren't even in among other aliens. Everyone in this shrinking universe seems to clamor for the same things (i.e., Gorbachev's dilemma). Everyone wants to watch *Dynasty*, everyone desires the same point of reference. Or do we?

Or is this another brazen example of Western culture's ongoing media hype?

I was born in Manila, Philippines, forty years ago; my upbringing was typically colonial and Catholic. All that was expected of me was that I finish my education and marry well, perhaps even to a non-Filipino. My mother was raised in even stricter circumstances; she longed to be a dancer, but ended up marrying at a young age, bearing three children, and taking up painting on the side. Her painting became another passion, and fortunately for me, she passed this passion for art in all its media down to me at an early age. My maternal grandfather was a writer and an accomplished political cartoonist and teacher, and so my family was not surprised when I decided at age eight that writing and theater were my life's work. No one tried to suppress my ambitions; I'm just not sure how seriously I was taken. The main thing, as in most families with female children, was that I marry a nice man and not embarrass anyone with my "art."

The implication was to make "nice" art, and not take any risks.

I was taught to look outside the indigenous culture for inspiration, taught that the label "Made in the USA" meant automatic superiority; in other words, like most colonized individuals, I was taught a negative image of myself. In school, classes were taught in English, Tagalog was taught as a foreign language (shouldn't this have been the other way around?), and the ways of the West were endlessly paraded and promoted. I sought escape in Tagalog melodramas and radio serials—especially our own lurid and wonderful Tagalog "Komiks"—but I was nevertheless drawn to Hollywood movies and the classics of Western literature. My lopsided education in Anglo ways was sophisticated; by the age of nine or ten, while enjoying the cheap thrills provided by adolescent Nancy Drew mysteries, I was already reading Walt Whitman, Emily and Charlotte Brontë, Honoré de Balzac, Edgar Allan Poe, Charles Dickens, and Jane Austen.

I spent my adolescent years in California, and studied theater arts at the American Conservatory Theater in San Francisco. The impact of finally moving to this environment was felt immediately. I was fourteen when I arrived, and I realized that, in spite of being female, it was perfectly all right for me to explore the city by myself. I started tentatively venturing out—long walks alone—and to my mother's horror, made it a habit. For those of you born and raised in America, this probably sounds ludicrous. I've seen children as young as ten or eleven (even younger) on public buses by themselves or with their friends. But in Manila, I was always protected and surrounded by older relatives or paid chaperones. It was unthinkable for a young girl to go to the movies by herself. It was a sin.

Perhaps what I value most in Western culture has been this profound sense of "freedom" as a woman—a freedom of movement and choice that is essential to any human being, and certainly essential for any writer. Freedom, of course, has its price.

While I have gotten used to this way of life in America, I straddle both worlds, like most urban Filipinos. When I speak of "home" even now, I refer to life *before* America, in that magical place of my childhood, the Philippines. Being of mixed parentage, I have family in Manila and the provinces, in California and the Midwest, and on my paternal side, family in Spain. In speaking of the Filipino American then, one also has to consider Hispanic roots, Chinese roots, etc. It is this hereditary mosaic that makes up the complex, unique, and dizzying Filipino culture. It is also this "elegant chaos" that definitely informs my work in style and the recurring themes of loss, yearning, alienation, rage, passion, and rebellion.

The actress Ching Valdes/Aran, herself a Filipina now living in New York, once said to me: "It took coming to America to actively Philippinize me." It is a sentiment probably many of us share.

The process of finding a writing "voice" that is true to one's self is often painful, but exhilarating and exciting as well. In the late 1960s and early 1970s, when I began publishing as a poet in San Francisco, I found empathy and revelation in the works of other Filipino writers who had settled in America (Carlos Bulosan, Bienvenido Santos, N.V.M. González), as well as Filipino American writers who were born and/or raised in America (Serafin Syquia, Lou Syquia, Oscar Peñaranda, Al Robles, Jocelyn Ignacio, Cyn Zarco, Norman Jayo, and others). I also discovered the poetic possibilities inherent in everyday speech and musical lyrics by reading and listening to Amiri Baraka, Ishmael Reed, Jayne Cortez, Al Young, Sonia Sanchez, The Last Poets, and my own colleagues, Thulani Davis and Ntozake Shange. Another peer who has really influenced my work is the Puerto Rican poet Victor Hernandez Cruz. Through his innovations, I freed myself to "dance" with my words.

Because I was always interested in writing fiction, I found solace and inspiration in the works of the South American masters: Gabriel

García Márquez, Manuel Puig, Luisa Valenzuela, and Guillermo Cabrera Infante. Their dark humor, poetic ironies, bilingual sophistication, pop culture references, surreal images, and fatalism were, for me, much closer to a Filipino sensibility than the contemporary writers I was also reading from other Asian cultures. Japanese writers can be very cool and restrained, whereas the Philippine and Latin American cultures share a more earthy "hothouse" sensibility.

Most urban Filipinos and Filipino Americans probably suffer from cultural schizophrenia, like I do. Hopefully, we will use this affliction to our advantage, for this post-colonial condition has its positive aspects. We need to turn the negative inside out, use it to enrich ourselves and our visions—for where would our extraordinary voices be without the outlaw rhythms of rock 'n' roll, the fractured lyricisms of jazz, the joyous gravity of salsa, the perverse fantasies of Hollywood, and our own epic melodramas?

Is there an Asian American aesthetic? Perhaps one exists insofar as influences that extend from the mother country (place of birth) and merge/clash with the influences of a pop culture that is universally perceived as "American" (i.e., North American). Some of these pop culture clichés include fashion and hence, dictate our self-image (jeans/black leather jackets/baseball caps); music (rock 'n' roll, black rap), which dictates the rhythms in our speech; TV (*The Cosby Show*), our notions of the model "minority." But in this shrinking universe, where white media appropriate black rappers, Asian ethnic fashion, and technology, and pretentious Zen car commercials find their way to television, who can really say Who is influencing Whom?

As Asian Americans, as writers and people of color in a world still dominated by Western thinking, it is vital that we straddle both cultures (East/West) and maintain our diversity and integrity. Writers and scholars have emerged in recent times (some familiar, some new) to continue to challenge the notion of a literature that encompasses the world—and reaffirms our existence in it. It is a multicultural vision that embraces and includes our shrinking universe; it is a multicultural vision that the white man fears and a vision that the rest of us can celebrate.

In the dark and futuristic movie *Blade Runner*, the image of a shrinking universe is shocking in its resemblance to society as we already know it. Los Angeles may be the capital in this version, but Japanese ads blink off and on, lighting up awesome electronic billboards, and street signs are posted in languages other than English. Where is the ubiquitous English language? Nowhere to be found. Nevertheless, this being Hollywood, everything is still run by the white man. In this movie, people of color belong to the underground, where they scurry and skulk in the rain, forever powerless, forever bit players in the big picture.

The difference in the art and literature that we are discussing is that it belongs to us. In the constant process of creating our work and re-creating ourselves, we acknowledge our roots as well as acknowledge the transformation that occurs living in the shadow of the dominant culture known as white America. Because of the racism that prevails, our work cannot afford to remain "small" or exclusive. If it is to survive and make a positive impact in a constantly evolving society, our work must address a universe as colored, confusing, magical, and terrifying as the one presented in Salman Rushdie's *The Satanic Verses*. I refer to this novel in particular because of the scope of its ambition, and because it confronts head-on a society of immigrants, aliens, others, natives, spirits, racists, angels, devils, and other sacred cows with courage, compassion, humor, and breathtaking genius. It may cost Salman Rushdie his life.

And the list of writers is growing (in no particular order): Bharati Mukherjee, Timothy Mo, Hanif Kureishi (who is British, but whose work accomplishes similar goals), Cynthia Kadohata, Fae Ng, Ninotchka Rosca, Shawn Wong, Amy Tan, Momoko Iko, Maxine Hong Kingston, Marilyn Chin, Garrett Hongo, Lawson Inada, Presco Tabios, Jeff Tagami and Shirley Ancheta, Kimiko Hahn, David Mura, Han Ong, Walter Lew, Laureen Mar, Alfred Yuson, David

Henry Hwang, Philip Gotanda, Daryl Chin, Trinh Minh-ha, Ko Won, Cathy Song, David Wong Louie, Nellie Wong, Wing Tek Lum, and so many others!

My novel *Dogeaters* was my attempt to make peace with the past and portray the beauty and richness of Philippine culture even in perilous times. I will probably write about the culture of exile and homesickness in one form or another until the day I die; it is my personal obsession, and it fuels my work.

In response to a recent interview on the question of Asian American identity and how it applies to my work in both literature and the theater, I described my writing (in poetry, theater, fiction, and film) as being populated by edgy characters who superficially seem to belong nowhere, but actually belong everywhere. It's my version of the "human" story.

It really doesn't matter if you're an immigrant or native-born, "F.O.B" (Fresh Off the Boat) or "A.B.C." (American Born Chinese), you're discovering who, what, and where you are all the time.

Another question I ask myself over and over again in my work: In what language do we dream?

Identity for me is not only racial, but sexual. I cannot think of myself as addressing the multicultural issue without including gender culture within the framework. We must respect the diversity of ethnic *and* sexual identity; for just as the Spanish version of guilt-ridden Christianity has influenced my psyche, and black and Latin music influences the rhythms of my characters' speech, then I happily acknowledge the wit and black-net veil of lyricism and doom which I have acquired from the works of homosexual writers like Tennessee Williams, Manuel Puig, and even Truman Capote.

It was a deliberate choice on my part to have one of my central characters in *Dogeaters* be a male prostitute who is half-black, half-Filipino—what one critic has called a "mongrel" child of the streets. My personal vision is very definitely a mongrel one, and I say this with pride.

In a recent essay on multiculturalism published in *Teachers & Writ-*

ers' Collaborative magazine, Christian McEwen refers to the distinguished novelist, scholar, and diplomat Carlos Fuentes: "For someone like Fuentes, skeptical, cosmopolitan, a Mexican national raised and educated in the United States, multiculturalism is more than an aesthetic or theoretical choice. It is a fierce personal necessity, a matter of political and cultural survival." This fierce personal necessity applies to our roles as Asian Americans, as writers, social thinkers, and people of color, and as citizens of the world.

michael dorris

michael dorris

Michael Dorris was born in 1945, in Louisville, Kentucky. He received a B.A. from Georgetown, and his M.Phil from Yale University. Until the late eighties, when he resigned to pursue his writing full-time, he was a professor of anthropology and chair of the Native American Studies department at Dartmouth. A powerful writer of fiction, nonfiction, and books for young adults, Dorris's publications include the novels *A Yellow Raft in Blue Water* and *The Crown of Columbus*, cowritten with his wife, Louise Erdrich; the short-story collection *Working Men; Paper Trail: Collected Essays, 1967–1992*; and *The Broken Cord: A Family's Ongoing Struggle with Fetal Alcohol Syndrome*, a wrenching personal account that won the National Book Critics Award in nonfiction. Dorris's book reviews and editorials appear frequently in newspapers around the country.

mixed blood

When we read books, especially when we're young, we're especially alert for things to recognize, clues to help us place ourselves in a confusing and daunting universe in which gender, age, economics, and identity itself are muddled by too much information, too many possibilities. We are externally ordered by one constellation in our immediate household, another in our social or school setting, many others on television. Where do we fit? What is the community of "us" to which we comfortably and securely and enduringly belong?

Such questions, I've always imagined, must be easier for some people to answer than they have been for me. Blond Lutheran Norwegian kids, growing up in Oslo, are clearly Norwegian. Oh sure, they're free to reject such a closed category, to become iconoclasts by embracing Mormonism or learning to love Thai food or cross-dressing as Swedes, but the base from which they operate, the thing they're desperate not to be in their rebellion—and therefore surely *are*—is Norwegian.

It's a trickier proposition if, like many Americans, we start off in ambiguity. When self-definition is contextually dictated or ascribed variously depending on who we're talking to, when a string of adjectives joined by hyphens prefixes our name in any introduction, and when, in terms of ethnic phenotypes, our eyes "look" this way, our accent sounds that way, our nose doesn't match our lips, and our hair texture is at odds with our skin pigmentation, we could be anyone—which translates, until we know better, into nobody at all.

I've spent too much of my life as one of those could-bes, torturously explaining to those bold or skeptical enough to ask how it is that

DNA-wise I'm a compound, an alloy, rather than an element. Early in my youth I learned that it was useful to have my complicated genealogy at the ready, available as a public service to be cross-checked, weighed, judged, and passed upon by people I barely knew but whose opinion on my pedigree, somehow, was supposed to matter. Around the house, among my relatives, I was simply me. In the outside world, I had to make the case.

Blah-blah-blah. My late father was Indian by way of and to varying degrees via both his parents, who themselves were also descended back through history from an occasional English or French ancestor. My mother is a union of rural Kentucky lace-curtain Irish and Indiana Swiss. My parents met and fell in love during World War II when my father was in the army and stationed at Fort Knox, and for a long set of complicated reasons, some of them ethnic-related, they had to go to California to get married. I had, as a result, a lot of relatives who were darker than I was, and a few who were lighter, and I could account for each feature of my being through reference to a different and color-coordinated gene pool. Some of my kinfolk were Roman Catholic, some weren't. None were rich, a few barely middle class, but the majority of whatever hue were poor. I felt, one way or another, at one time or another, equally comfortable or uncomfortable living on a reservation, in a city, on a farm—and because of my immediate family's economic situation, I seemed to stay in no place long enough to fully blend in. Satisfied?

All this palaver usually made me anxious, then bored, then angry. It was so much preamble, a kind of endless Japanese etiquette ceremony that preceded real encounter, a repetitious ritual that, more than anything else, ultimately inspired me, during my teens, to either say an instant "yes, you're right" to the first guess a perfect stranger might throw out as to who or what I "really" was, or to stay home. Sometimes it still does.

And what did I do at home, with no resident siblings and often living too far out of town to walk to a friend's house? I read. Everything. I read my grandfather's slim volumes of Victorian poetry, my mother's

Good Housekeeping magazines, the Hardy Boys mysteries, old *National Geographics*. I read cookbooks, newspapers, the ads in the back of *Popular Mechanics*, and hundreds of comic books. I read about the lives of the saints, the betrayals of Osceola and Crazy Horse, the adventures of *A Connecticut Yankee at King Arthur's Court*. And much as I enjoyed and learned from it all, hard as I looked without truly realizing what I was looking for, I never, not once, found myself.

Everybody I encountered in literature simply was unequivocally who they were—even the Green Lantern, depending on necessity, was either kelly green or picket-fence white, never a nice pastel. Nobody, unless one counted *The Prince and the Pauper*—who, after all, knew the hidden truth of their clear situation all along—ever just *wasn't*. Where were my role models? Where was Helen, Half-Breed Hunkpapa of Houston, or Murray, the Mixed-Blood Maverick, leaping conflicting ethnicities in a single, effortless bound? Look, up in the sky! It's both a bird *and* a plane! It's Super-Combo!

The absence of fictional or biographical protagonists possessed of a bi- or triracial background is curious because by its very nature multiple relatedness is dramatic and interesting. A character with an insider's knowledge of more than one group is potentially an ideal guide, both objective and subjective, sufficiently well informed to know the right questions to ask but detached enough to still be surprised at the answers. Persons linked to a broad and disparate network of culture can match the solutions reached at one place to the problems faced by another. Their very marginality requires that they listen more sharply, use words with care and precision, watch closely in order to learn how to behave. They can easily stand as a metaphor for the dislocations of children in an adult world, for a boy who finds himself among girls (or vice versa), for a city kid stranded in the country. Inasmuch as they must grapple as often with alienation as with affinity, mixed-bloods mirror the perplexity of every human being who must constantly pass from a seemingly stable state—childhood—into the flux of maturity. Their very resistance to facile definition renders them, in the end, more typical of human reality than people whose apparent stability in a monochrome identity is a fleeting illusion, an unsustainable luxury.

I've tried to give positive voice to this condition in my own writing. Rayona, in *A Yellow Raft in Blue Water* (1987), overhears her Native American mother talking to her African-American father:

> "We're the wrong color for each other," I heard Mom tell him a long time ago. "That's what your friends think."
>
> "We may be different shades but look at the blend." Dad's voice had been low, almost singing. He probably wasn't talking about me, but he might have been, since my skin is a combination of theirs. Once, in a hardware store, I found each of our exact shades on a paint mix-tone chart. Mom was Almond Joy, Dad was Burnt Clay, and I was Maple Walnut.

Or, in *The Crown of Columbus* (1991), Louise Erdrich and I let the feisty Vivian Twostar proclaim:

> "I belong to the lost tribe of mixed bloods, that hodgepodge amalgam of hue and cry that defies easy placement. When the DNA of my various ancestors . . . combined to form me, the result was not some genteel, undecipherable puree that comes from a Cuisinart. You know what they say on the side of the Bisquick box, under instructions for pancakes? Mix with fork. Leave lumps. That was me. . . . 'Caught between two worlds,' is the way we're often characterized, but I'd put it differently. We are the *catch*."

Brave words, Viv, but sell that one to me at age eleven, self-conscious about my light complexion at a powwow or listening, embarrassed and tongue-tied, while oblivious to half of my background all-white schoolmates tell cruel jokes about drunken Indians.

Growing up mixed-blood is, for too many of us and for too long in our lives, growing up mixed up. Dual identity may eventually be an advantage for empathy, may greatly benefit us if we become a psychiatrist or a writer or a counselor, but while it's happening it's usually not much fun. It demands wariness, humility, patience, and the lonely nurturing of a self-image strong enough to stand up to all challengers, whether intentionally malevolent or merely stupid. It inspires our jealousy toward those who don't seem to face the same problems we do because they look the way we feel, and simultaneous guilt because they often suffer or are discriminated against for that very otherwise enviable quality. It engenders instant recognition for and psychological bonding with another person of any age going through a similar trial. It wears us out even as we tell ourselves it builds character. It insists that we create an independent model for who and how we need honestly to be, then follow it because, finally and forever, for better or worse, mixed and stirred up is who we are.

richard rodriguez

richard rodriguez

Richard Rodriguez was born in 1944 in San Francisco and grew up in Sacramento. Growing up in a Spanish-speaking family, Rodriguez knew only fifty words of English when he began school. He went on to study at Stanford University, Columbia University, the University of California, Berkeley, and with the help of a Fullbright Fellowship studied at the British Museum in London.

Rodriguez's now classic autobiography, *Hunger of Memory: The Education of Richard Rodriguez*, marked him as one of the most elegant and insightful writers of his generation. He is also the author of the powerful collection of essays, *Days of Obligation: An Argument with My Mexican Father*. Rodriguez, who now lives in San Francisco, has carved out a place for himself as a fiercely independent thinker who places his own experience under examination, rendering in exquisite testimony what it means to be a man brimming with original observations, ideas, and questions.

asians

For the child of immigrant parents, the knowledge comes like a slap: America exists.

America exists everywhere in the city—on billboards; frankly in the smell of burgers and French fries. America exists in the slouch of the crowd, the pacing of the traffic lights, the assertions of neon, the cry of freedom overriding the nineteenth-century melodic line.

Grasp the implications of American democracy in a handshake or in a stranger's Jeffersonian "hi." America is irresistible. Nothing to do with choosing.

Our parents came to America for the choices America offers. What the child of immigrant parents knows is that here is inevitability.

A Chinese boy says his high school teacher is always after him to stand up, speak up, look up. Yeah, but then his father puts him down at home: "Since when have you started looking your father in the eye?"

I'd like you to meet Jimmy Lamm. Mr. Lamm was an architect in Saigon. Now he is a cabbie in San Francisco. Stalled in traffic in San Francisco, Jimmy tells me about the refugee camp in Guam where, for nearly two years, he and his family were quartered before their flight to America. A teenager surfs by on a skateboard, his hair cresting in purple spikes like an iron crown, his freedom as apparent, as deplorable, as Huck Finn's.

Damn kid. Honk. Honk.

The damn kid howls with pleasure. Flips us the bird.

Do you worry that your children will end up with purple hair?

Silence.

Then Jimmy says his children have too much respect for the struggle he and his wife endured. His children would never betray him so.

On the floor of Jimmy Lamm's apartment, next to the television, is a bowl of fruit and a burning wand of joss.

He means: His children would never *choose* to betray him.

Immigrant parents re-create a homeland in the parlor, tacking up postcards or calendars of some impossible blue—lake or sea or sky.

The child of immigrant parents is supposed to perch on a hyphen, taking only the dose of America he needs to advance in America.

At the family picnic, the child wanders away from the spiced food and faceless stories to watch some boys playing baseball in the distance.

My Mexican father still regards America with skepticism from the high window of his morning paper. "Too much freedom," he says. Though he has spent most of his life in this country, my father yet doubts such a place as the United States of America exists. He cannot discern boundaries. How else to describe a country?

My father admires a flower bed on a busy pedestrian street in Zurich—he holds up the *National Geographic* to show me. "You couldn't have that in America," my father says.

When I was twelve years old, my father said he wished his children had Chinese friends—so polite, so serious are Chinese children in my father's estimation. The Spanish word he used was *formal*.

I didn't have any Chinese friends. My father did. Seventh and J Street was my father's Orient. My father made false teeth for several Chinese dentists downtown. When a Chinese family tried to move in a few blocks away from our house, I heard a friend's father boast that the neighbors had banded together to "keep out the Japs."

Many years pass.

In college, I was reading *The Merchant of Venice*—Shylock urging his daughter to avoid the temptation of the frivolous Christians on the Lido. Come away from the window, Shylock commands. I heard my father's voice:

Hear you me, Jessica.
Lock up my doors, and when you hear the drum
And the vile squealing of the wry-necked fife,
Clamber not you up to the casements then,
Nor thrust your head into the public street
To gaze on Christian fools with varnished faces,
But stop my house's ears, I mean my casements.
Let not the sound of shallow foppery enter
My sober house.

I interview the mother on Evergreen Street for the *Los Angeles Times*. The mother says they came from Mexico ten years ago, and—look—already they have this nice house. Each year the kitchen takes on a new appliance.

Outside the door is Los Angeles; in the distance, the perpetual orbit of traffic. Here old women walk slowly under paper parasols, past the Vietnam vet who pushes his tinkling ice-cream cart past little green lawns, little green lawns, little green lawns. (Here teenagers have black scorpions tattooed into their biceps.)

Children here are fed and grow tall. They love Christmas. They laugh at cartoons. They go off to school with children from Vietnam, from Burbank, from Hong Kong. They get into fights. They come home and they say dirty words. Aw, Ma, they say. Gimme a break, they say.

The mother says she does not want American children. It is the thing about Los Angeles she fears, the season of adolescence, of Huck Finn and Daisy Miller.

Foolish mother. She should have thought of that before she came. She will live to see that America takes its meaning from adolescence. She will have American children.

The best metaphor of America remains the dreadful metaphor—the Melting Pot. Fall into the Melting Pot, ease into the Melting Pot, or jump into the Melting Pot—it makes no difference—you will find yourself a stranger to your parents, a stranger to your own memory of yourself.

A Chinese girl walks to the front of the classroom, unfolds several ruled pages, and begins to read her essay to a trio of judges (I am one of her judges).

The voice of the essay is the voice of an immigrant. Stammer and elision approximate naiveté (the judges squirm in their chairs). The narrator remembers her nightlong journey to the United States aboard a Pan Am jet. The moon. Stars. Then a memory within a memory: In the darkened cabin of the plane, sitting next to her sleeping father, the little girl remembers bright China.

Many years pass.

The narrator's voice hardens into an American voice; her diction takes on rock and chrome. There is an ashtray on the table. The narrator is sitting at a sidewalk cafe in San Francisco. She is sixteen years old. She is with friends. The narrator notices a Chinese girl passing on the sidewalk. The narrator remembers bright China. The passing girl's face turns toward hers. The narrator recognizes herself in the passing girl—herself less assimilated. Their connective glance lasts only seconds. The narrator is embarrassed by her double—she remembers the cabin of the plane, her sleeping father, the moon, stars. The stranger disappears.

End of essay.

The room is silent as the Chinese student raises her eyes from the text.

One judge breaks the silence. Do you think your story is a sad story?

No, she replies. It is a true story.

What is the difference?

(Slowly, then.)

When you hear a sad story you cry, she says. When you hear a true story, you cry even more.

• • •

The U.S. Army took your darling boy, didn't they? With all his allergies and his moles and his favorite flavors. And when they gave him back, the crystals of his eyes had cracked. You weren't sure if this was the right baby. The only other institution as unsentimental and as subversive of American individuality has been the classroom.

In the nineteenth century, even as the American city was building, Samuel Clemens romanced the nation with a celebration of the wildness of the American river, the eternal rejection of school and shoes. But in the red-brick cities, and on streets without trees, the river became an idea, a learned idea, a shared idea, a civilizing idea, taking all to itself. Women, usually women, stood in front of rooms crowded with the children of immigrants, teaching those children a common language. For language is not just another classroom skill, as today's bilingualists would have it. Language is *the* lesson of grammar school. And from the schoolmarm's achievement came the possibility of a shared history and a shared future. To my mind, this achievement of the nineteenth-century classroom was an honorable one, comparable to the opening of the plains, the building of bridges. Grammar school teachers forged a nation.

A century later, my own teachers encouraged me to read *Huckleberry Finn*. I tried several times. My attempts were frustrated by the dialect voices. (*"You don't know about me without you have read . . ."*) There was, too, a confidence in Huck I shied away from and didn't like and wouldn't trust. The confidence was America.

Eventually, but this was many years after, I was able to read in Huck's dilemma—how he chafed so in autumn—a version of my own fear of the classroom: Huck as the archetypal bilingual child. And, later still, I discerned in Huck a version of the life of our nation.

This nation was formed from a fear of the crowd. Those early Puritans trusted only the solitary life. Puritans advised fences. Build a fence around all you hold dear and respect other fences. Protestantism taught Americans to believe that America does not exist—not as a culture, not as shared experience, not as a communal reality. Because of Protestantism, the American *ideology* of individualism is always at war with the experience of our lives, our *culture*. As long as we reject the notion of culture, we are able to invent the future.

Lacking any plural sense of ourselves, how shall we describe Americanization except as loss? The son of Italian immigrant parents is no longer Italian. America is the country where one stops being Italian or Chinese or German.

And yet notice the testimony of thousands of bellhops in thousands of hotel lobbies around the world: Americans exist. There is a recognizable type—the accent, of course; the insecure tip; the ready smile; the impatience; the confidence of an atomic bomb informing every gesture.

When far from home, Americans easily recognize one another in a crowd. It is only when we return home, when we live and work next to one another, that Americans choose to believe anew in the fact of our separateness.

Americans have resorted to the idea of a shared culture only at times of international competition, at times of economic depression, during war, during periods of immigration. Nineteenth-century nativists feared Catholics and Jews would undermine the Protestant idea of America. As the nineteenth-century American city crowded with rag pickers, and crucifix-kissers, and garlic-eaters, yes, and as metaphors of wildness attached to the American city, nativists consoled themselves with a cropped version of America—the small white town, the general store, the Elks Hall, the Congregational church.

To this day, political journalists repair to the "heartland" to test the rhetoric of Washington or New York against true America.

But it was the antisociability of American Protestantism which paradoxically allowed for an immigrant nation. Lacking a communal sense, how could Americans resist the coming of strangers? America became a multiracial, multireligious society precisely because a small band of Puritans did not want the world.

The American city became the fame of America worldwide.

In time, the American city became the boast of America. In time, Americans would admit their country's meaning resided in the city.

America represented freedom—the freedom to leave Europe behind, the freedom to re-create one's life, the freedom to re-create the world. In time, Americans came to recognize themselves in the immigrant—suitcase in hand, foreign-speaking, bewildered by the city. The figure of the immigrant became, like the American cowboy, a figure of loneliness, and we trusted that figure as descriptive of Protestant American experience. We are a nation of immigrants, we were able to say.

Now "Hispanics and Asians" have replaced "Catholics and Jews" in the imaginations of nativists. The nativist fear is that non-European immigrants will undo the European idea of America (forgetting that America was formed against the idea of Europe).

We are a nation of immigrants—most of us say it easily now. And we are working on a new cliché to accommodate new immigrants: The best thing about immigrants, the best that they bring to America, we say, is their "diversity." We mean they are not us—the Protestant creed.

In the late nineteenth century, when much of San Francisco was sand dunes, city fathers thought to plant a large park running out to the edge of the sea. Prescient city fathers. San Francisco would become crowded. Someday there would be the need for a park at the edge of the sea.

Having reached the end of the continent, Americans contemplated finitude. The Pacific Coast was ominous to the California imagination. The Pacific Coast was an Asian horizon. The end of us was the beginning of them. Old duffers warned, "Someday there will be sampans in the harbor."

With one breath people today speak of Hispanics and Asians—the new Americans. Between the two, Asians are the more admired—the model minority—more Protestant than Protestants; so hardworking, self-driven; so bright. But the Asian remains more unsettling to American complacence, because the Asian is culturally more foreign.

Hispanics may be reluctant or pushy or light or dark, but Hispanics are recognizably European. They speak a European tongue. They worship or reject a European God. The shape of the meat they eat is identifiable. But the Asian?

Asians rounded the world for me. I was a Mexican teenager in America who had become an Irish Catholic. When I was growing up in the 1960s, I heard Americans describing their nation as simply bipartite: black and white. When black and white America argued, I felt I was overhearing some family quarrel that didn't include me. Korean and Chinese and Japanese faces in Sacramento rescued me from the simplicities of black and white America.

I was in high school when my uncle from India died, my Uncle Raj, the dentist. After Raj died, we went to a succession of Chinese dentists, the first Asian names I connected with recognizable faces; the first Asian hands.

In the 1960s, whole blocks of downtown Sacramento were to be demolished for a redevelopment. The *Sacramento Bee* reported several Chinese businessmen had declared their intention to build a ten-story office building downtown with a pagoda roof. About that same time, there was another article in the *Bee*. Mexican entrepreneurs would turn Sixth and K into a Mexican block with cobblestones, restaurants, colonial facades. My father was skeptical concerning the Mexican enterprise. "Guess which one will never get built?" my father intoned from the lamplight, snapping the spine of his newspaper.

Dr. Chiang, one of our family dentists, had gone to the University of the Pacific. He encouraged the same school for me. Our entire conversational motif, repeated at every visit, was college—his path and my plans.

Then there was Dr. Wang.

Not Dr. Wang! My sister refused. Dr. Wang didn't bother with Novocain. Dr. Wang's office was a dark and shabby place.

My father said we owed it to Dr. Wang to be his patients. Dr. Wang referred business to my father.

Dr. Wang joked about my long nose. "Just like your father." And again: "Just like your father," as he pulled my nose up to open my mouth. Then China entered my mouth in a blast of garlic, a whorl of pain.

The Chinese businessmen built a ten-story office building downtown with a pagoda roof. Just as my father predicted they would.

Americans must resist the coming of fall, the starched shirt, the inimical expectation of the schoolmarm, because Americans want to remain individual. The classroom will teach us a language in common. The classroom will teach a history that implicates us with others. The classroom will tell us that we belong to a culture.

American educators, insofar as they are Americans, share with their students a certain ambivalence, even a resistance, to the public lessons of school. Witness the influence of progressivism on American education, a pedagogy that describes the primary purpose of education as fostering independence of thought, creativity, originality—notions that separate one student from another.

The hardest lesson for me, as for Huck Finn, as for the Chinese kid in the fifth paragraph of this chapter, was the lesson of public identity. What I needed from the classroom was a public life. The earliest necessity for any student is not individuality but something closer to the reverse. With Huck, I needed to learn the names of British kings and dissident Protestants, because they were the beginning of us. I read the writings of eighteenth-century white men who powdered their wigs and kept slaves, because these were the men who shaped the country that shaped my life.

Today, Huck Finn would emerge as the simple winner in the contest of public education. Today, Huck's schoolmarm would be cried down by her students as a tyrannical supremacist.

American educators have lost the confidence of their public institution. The failure represents, in part, an advance for America: the advance of the postwar black civil rights movement. As America became racially integrated, the black civil rights movement encouraged a romantic secession from the idea of America—Americans competed with one another to claim victimization for themselves, some fence for themselves as minorities.

A second factor undermining the classroom's traditional function has been the large, non-European immigration of the last two decades. It was one thing to imagine a common culture when most immigrants came from Europe. A grammar school teacher in California may now have students from fifty-four language groups in her class, as does one grammar school teacher I know. How shall she teach such an assembly anything singular?

Or the college professor who lectures on Shakespeare. Most of his students are Asian. He was grading papers on *The Merchant of Venice* last term when he suddenly realized most of his Asian students had no idea what it meant that Shylock was a Jew.

Teachers and educational bureaucrats bleat in chorus: We are a nation of immigrants. The best that immigrants bring to America is diversity. American education should respect diversity, celebrate diversity. Thus the dilemma of our national diversity becomes (with a little choke on logic) the solution to itself. But diversity is a liquid noun. Diversity admits everything, stands for nothing.

There are influential educators today, and I have met them, who believe the purpose of American education is to instill in children a pride in their ancestral pasts. Such a curtailing of education seems to me condescending, seems to me the worst sort of missionary spirit. Did anyone attempt to protect the white middle-class student of yore from the ironies of history? Thomas Jefferson—that great democrat—was also a slave owner. Need we protect black students from complexity? Thomas Jefferson, that slave owner, was also a democrat. American history has become a pageant of exemplary slaves and black educators. Gay studies, women's studies, ethnic studies—the new curriculum ensures that education will be flattering. But I submit that America is not a tale for sentimentalists.

If I am a newcomer to your country, why teach me about my ancestors? I need to know about seventeenth-century Puritans in order to make sense of the rebellion I notice everywhere in the American city.

Teach me about mad British kings so I will understand the American penchant for iconoclasm. Then teach me about cowboys and Indians; I should know that tragedies created the country that will create me.

Once you toss out Benjamin Franklin and Andrew Jackson, you toss out Navajos. You toss out immigrant women who worked the sweatshops of the Lower East Side. Once you toss out Thomas Jefferson, you toss out black history.

A high school principal tells me there are few black students in his school, but—oh my!—in the last decade his school has changed its color, changed its accent; changed memory. Instead of Black History Week, his school now observes "Newcomers' Week." But does not everyone in America have a stake in black history? To be an American is to belong to black history.

To argue for a common culture is not to propose an exclusionary culture or a static culture. The classroom is always adding to the common text, because America is a dynamic society. Susan B. Anthony, Martin Luther King, Jr., are inducted into the textbook much as they are canonized by the U.S. Postal Service, not as figures of diversity but as persons who implicate our entire society.

Sherlock Holmes?

I know a lot of teachers. Yet another teacher faces an eighth-grade class of Filipino immigrants. Boy-oh-boy, she would sure like to watch me try to teach her eighth-grade Filipino students to read Conan Doyle.

For example, she says: Meerschaum—a kind of pipe. Well, a pipe—you know, you smoke? Pen knife. Bell pull. Harley Street. Hobnail boots. Dressing gown. Fez. Cockney. Turkish delight. Pall Mall. Wales . . . Well, they know what whales are, she says mordantly. It's too hard. It's too hard for Conan Doyle, that's for damn sure.

But for Shakespeare?

A high school counselor tells me her school will soon be without a football team. Too few whites and blacks are enrolled; Hispanic and Asian kids would rather play soccer. As I listen to her, a thought occurs to me: She hates football. She looks for the demise of football.

Perhaps what she wants most from Hispanic and Asian children is the same reassurance earlier generations of Americans sought from European immigrants, the reassurance—the hope—that an immigrant can undo America, can untie the cultural knot.

Now the American university is dismantling the American canon in my name. In the name of my father, in the name of Chinese grocers and fry cooks and dentists, the American university disregards the Judeo-Christian foundation of the American narrative. The white university never asked my father whether or not his son should read Milton, of course. Hispanics and Asians have become the convenient national excuse for the accomplishment of what America has always wanted done—the severing of memory, the dismantlement of national culture. The end of history.

Americans are lonely now. Hispanics and Asians represent to us the alternatives of communal cultures at a time when Americans are demoralized. Americans are no longer sure that economic invincibility derives from individualism. Look at Japan! Americans learn chopsticks. Americans lustily devour what they say they fear to become. Sushi will make us lean, corporate warriors. Mexican Combination Plate #3, smothered in mestizo gravy, will burn a hole through our hearts.

No belief is more cherished by Americans, no belief is more typical of America, than the belief that one can choose to be free of American culture. One can pick and choose. Learn Spanish. Study Buddhism. . . . My Mexican father was never so American as when he wished his children might cultivate Chinese friends.

Many years pass.

Eventually I made my way through *Huckleberry Finn*. I was, by that time, a graduate student of English, able to trail Huck and Jim through thickets of American diction and into a clearing. Sitting in a university library, I saw, once more, the American river.

There is a discernible culture, a river, a thread, connecting Thomas Jefferson to Lucille Ball to Malcolm X to Sitting Bull. The panhandler at one corner is related to the pamphleteer at the next, who is related to the bank executive who is related to the Punk wearing a fuck u T-shirt. The immigrant child sees this at once. But then he is encouraged to forget the vision.

When I was a boy who spoke Spanish, I saw America whole. I realized that there was a culture here because I lived apart from it. I didn't like America. Then I entered the culture. I entered the culture as you did, by going to school. I became Americanized. I ended up believing in choices as much as any of you do.

What my best teachers realized was their obligation to pass on to their students a culture in which the schoolmarm is portrayed as a minor villain.

When I taught Freshman English at Berkeley, I took the "F" bus from San Francisco. This was about the time when American educators were proclaiming Asians to be "whiz kids" and Asian academic triumphs fed the feature pages of American newspapers. There were lots of Asians on the "F" bus.

One day, sitting next to a Chinese student on the bus, I watched him study. The way he worried over the text was troubling to me. He knew something about the hardness of life, the seriousness of youth, that America had never taught me. I turned away; I looked out the bus window; I got off the bus at my usual stop. But consider the two of us on the "F" bus headed for Berkeley: the Chinese student poring over his text against some terrible test. Me sitting next to him, my briefcase full of English novels; lucky me. The Asian and the Hispanic. We represented, so many Americans then imagined, some new force in America, a revolutionary change, an undoing of the European line. But it was not so.

Immigrant parents send their children to school (simply, they think) to acquire the skills to "survive" in America. But the child returns home as America. Foolish immigrant parents.

By eight o'clock that morning—the morning of the bus ride—I stood, as usual, in a classroom in Wheeler Hall, lecturing on tragedy and comedy. Asian kids at the back of the room studied biochemistry, as usual, behind propped-up Shakespeares. I said nothing, made no attempt to recall them. At the end of the hour, I announced to the class that, henceforward, class participation would be a consideration in grading. Asian eyes peered over the blue rims of their Oxford Shakespeares.

Three Asian students came to my office that afternoon. They were polite. They had come to ask about the final exam—what did they need to know?

They took notes. Then one student (I would have said the most Americanized of the three) spoke up: "We think, Mr. Rodriguez, that you are prejudiced against Asian students. Because we do not speak up in class."

I made a face. Nonsense, I blustered. Freshman English is a course concerned with language. Is it so unreasonable that I should expect students to speak up in class? One Asian student is the best student in class . . . and so forth.

I don't remember how our meeting concluded. I recall my deliberation when I gave those three grades. And I think now the students were just. I did have a bias, an inevitable American bias, that favored the talkative student. Like most other American teachers, I equated intelligence with liveliness or defiance.

Another Asian student, a woman, an ethnic Chinese student from Vietnam or Cambodia, ended up with an F in one of my classes. It wasn't that she had no American voice, or even that she didn't know what to make of Thoreau. She had missed too many classes. She didn't even show up for the Final.

On a foggy morning during winter break, this woman came to my office with her father to remonstrate.

I was too embarrassed to look at her. I spoke to her father. She sat by the door.

I explained the five essay assignments. I showed him my grade book, the blank spaces next to her name. The father and I both paused a long time over my evidence. I suggested the university's remedial writing course . . . *Really, you know, your counselor should never have . . .*

In the middle of my apology, he stood up; he turned and walked to where his daughter sat. I could see only his back as he hovered over her. I heard the slap. He moved away.

And then I saw her. She was not crying. She was looking down at her hands composed neatly on her lap.

Jessica!

ira
glasser
audre
lorde

II
talking race

john
powell
peggy
mcintosh
bharati
mukherjee
reverend
cecil b.
williams
henry
louis
gates, jr.

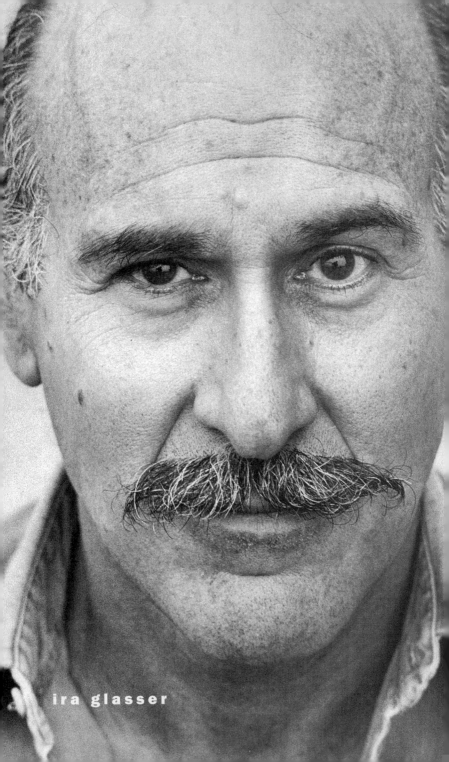

ira glasser

ira
glasser

Ira Glasser was born in Brooklyn, New York, in 1938. He attended
Queens College of the City of New York, Ohio State University, and the
New School for Social Research. He has been executive director of the
American Civil Liberties Union since 1978. Prior to his association with
the ACLU, Glasser was a mathematician and a member of the science
and mathematics faculties at Queens College and Sarah Lawrence
College.

Glasser's writings include: *Visions of Liberty: The Bill of Rights for All
Americans*, and the coauthored, *Doing Good: The Limits of
Benevolence*. His essays on civil liberties issues have appeared in the
New York Times, the *Village Voice, Harper's*, the *New Republic*, and the
Nation. Glasser brings intelligence, purpose, and a keen sense of
history to the discussion of race in America. He is a marvelous speaker,
not of the rousing soapbox variety but of coherent vision and genuine
leadership. The following speech, given informally without notes, may be
the best forty-five-minute history of American race relations that we
have.

Married and the father of four children, Glasser lives in New York.

civil rights and civil liberties

Part of the difficulty for my generation in talking about race is that we grew up at a time when race was the number one civil liberties problem. The problem of inequality of rights; the fact that virtually every right was disproportionately violated for people of color, and particularly for blacks, made civil rights the consuming problem of my youth. And it was a problem that many of us approached with uncommon and unjustified optimism. We really thought that we were going to fix it in our lifetime. I suppose that everybody that is eighteen brings that optimism to bear on their chosen issues and comes to grief later. But let me begin at the beginning, because too often we don't begin there, and I think that it's always important to take note of.

Slavery is the original sin of this country. Like original sin in Catholic theology, it is extremely difficult, perhaps impossible, to wash away. This country was born in slavery. The founders who, in other respects, were apostles of liberty believed and spoke with great passion against the Stamp Act, which put a three-penny tax on all of their goods, declaring it the equivalent of slavery. They fought a revolution over the Stamp Act while at the same time accepting real chattel slavery in their midst. They were not a generation of people who didn't see it. They were not good Germans who were able to claim that they did not know what was going on. They were not even able to claim they could justify it. But they were willing to tolerate it. They were willing to buy into it. To codify it, to make it part of the bargain of starting the new country. So the country was born with the blood of slavery as an integral part of its bones.

We need to come to terms with this history. We need to understand that the problems facing African-Americans in being absorbed into the American culture are distinct from every other immigrant group. Nobody else came here except willingly. For almost everybody else, arriving on the shores of America represented escape from tyranny, and enhanced freedom, even if a struggle with poverty ensued. Coming to the United States meant an increase in freedom and an increase in equality, even if it involved a terrible struggle with economic deprivation. But for African-Americans it represented, as we know, quite the opposite. All talk of race today has to begin with this fact.

The Bill of Rights and the independent court system were marvelous inventions which nobody else in the world had. The Bill of Rights was designed to guarantee all of us certain rights against the government. An independent court system of judges appointed for life, so that they would not be subject to the momentary hysteria of a democratic system, would enforce the Bill of Rights even against democratic wishes. That is what rights are—legal protections against the majority. If the majority is men, the Bill of Rights protects women; if the majority is whites, the Bill of Rights protects blacks; if the majority are Catholics, the Bill of Rights protects Jews; if the majority are Judeo-Christians, the Bill of Rights protects Muslims.

Of course nobody was talking about blacks then, they weren't part of the picture, they weren't part of the Bill of Rights, they weren't human. That's what accepting slavery meant. It wasn't just that these were people who were on the bottom of an economic ladder. In order to justify slavery you had to internalize the fact that they weren't human. And not being human, they were not included in the definition of the people, or in all of the declarations of equality and rights contained in the beautiful language of the Declaration of Independence and the Bill of Rights and the Constitution.

One of the things the founders forgot is that although the judiciary was independent once it was appointed, the appointment process itself was political, and the people were appointed out of the culture in which they lived. So while you had independent judges, they were all white men. They didn't give women the right to vote. It took 130 years, two thirds of our bicentennial period, before women had the right to vote. And they didn't do it because the Supreme Court gave it to them applying the equality guarantees of the Fourteenth Amendment. They did it because they made a nuisance of themselves in the streets for seventy years and forced a constitutional amendment. Blacks were not in the Bill of Rights altogether, and those folks who were the independent judges certainly were not going to apply any of the Bill of Rights to them. And, in fact, the Supreme Court didn't apply the Bill of Rights for much of anything in the first hundred years.

In 1857 the Supreme Court struck down a federal law in the Dred Scott decision, when they actually, in the only time they ever ruled on slavery, upheld it. So that well into the nineteenth century, to the extent that the courts worked at all, they were part of the problem; they were not part of the solution.

When the Dred Scott decision came down it was greeted by the two leading Abolitionists of the day—one white, [William] Lloyd Garrison, and one black, Frederick Douglass—in much the same way. Douglass said we should greet this decision cheerfully because it may lead to a political movement that finally overturns the entire enterprise of slavery. And Garrison said much the same thing. He said we must greet this decision with what he called—a wonderful phrase—"a tremendous excitement." And of course the tremendous excitement that turned out to make both Garrison and Douglass accurate predictors of what would happen was the Civil War.

The Civil War finally put an end to slavery and in its wake there was reconstruction. The Thirteenth Amendment abolishing slavery constitutionally, which should have happened at the beginning, finally happened. The Fourteenth Amendment, which guaranteed equal protection of the laws against state governments, was passed. The Fifteenth Amendment, which barred discrimination in voting on the basis of race, was passed. And a whole host of civil rights laws was passed for the first time in the history of the country to implement those constitutional rights. Blacks were elected to state legislatures and some to Congress. There was even talk of forty acres and a mule, which would redistribute enough wealth so that blacks, who had once been property, could now own property.

None of that, of course, lasted very long, as we know. Progress, as always, created an enormous political reaction. First the courts were the villain. They basically destroyed the Fourteenth Amendment by interpretation in a way that was really not restored until the 1960s, nearly a century later. They struck down all, or mostly all, of the civil rights laws as unconstitutional in the same way that they upheld slavery before the Civil War.

In the Dred Scott decision the Chief Justice of the United States Supreme Court said, in justifying slavery, that blacks in this country had no rights that whites were bound to respect. The decisions that eviscerated the Fourteenth Amendment and struck down the civil rights laws in the post-Reconstruction period didn't say it quite so bluntly, but it amounted to the same thing.

Pretty soon the political culture reasserted itself, the way the grass retakes a road that you've chopped through a jungle. Once the protection of the Fourteenth Amendment and the civil rights laws were taken away by the courts, state law reasserted itself in the South. The Klan began to run wild. Violence became endemic. What previously had been enforced by the tradition of slavery was now enforced through state-sanctioned terror.

The only thing that stood in the way was the presence of federal troops, and in 1877, President Rutherford B. Hayes removed the federal troops in what represented a last political cave-in to the reactionary response to racial progress. This series of events that unraveled reconstruction and reasserted a system of subjugation and subordination in the southern states was no temporary setback. No progress is linear. You don't just keep climbing up that ladder. There is not an issue in the world in which you do not go forward two steps and back one step. But this was not simply a momentary setback in that upward progression. This was a setback so thorough, so pervasive, so complete, so fundamental, that it ushered in another hundred years of state-sanctioned terror and subjugation enforced by terror in the states of the South. And once again the country tolerated it. It was not despite the Supreme Court, it was led by the Supreme Court. It was not despite Congress, it was led by Congress. It was not despite the president, it was led by the president.

It was as if that original sin was too much to overcome. All those restorative and redemptive things that happened after the Civil War were swept away easily, it seemed. And blacks once again found themselves in a completely powerless and vulnerable and terrifying position. A position that was really not improved for another hundred years.

That whole stage is part of our history that we have to understand when we talk about the problem today. It is never far from us. It is a history of which too many people are ignorant or regard as safely over. We must deal with our heritage.

A country that tolerates racial discrimination against blacks at the same time that it professes to stand for equal rights for everybody can only deal with the dissonance if at some level it believes that blacks are less than human. That they exist outside the normal protections. You either have to give up a fundamental value—that we believe in equal justice and equal rights for everybody—or you have to convince yourself, even at a subconscious level, that you're not giving it up, because these people to whom you have denied those equal rights are not fully human. Once that gets ingrained in the culture, it is very hard to get out. That is what I mean by original sin.

We can read the history books, we can read the case law, we can read about what Congress did and what the president did and all the lynching. What we cannot read is what went on in people's minds. What we cannot read is the way children were raised, what they heard around the dinner table and what they didn't hear. And the kind of things that were said privately but never publicly, even among people who professed not to like this.

I grew up in the liberal North in a liberal Jewish family where it was part of growing up to hear racist remarks at every wedding, at every family gathering. Not from everybody, and often not without other people from the family getting into arguments about it. But it was the kind of thing that none of those people would have ever said publicly. These were people who sent contributions in the years later to Martin Luther King, Jr., at the same time that they continued to live where there were no blacks, to send their kids to school where there were no blacks, to keep their abstract beliefs away from their real lives. This kind of schizophrenia was internalized, and justified by the belief that it was okay because, after all, blacks weren't like us.

Then, of course, we fought World War II against that very ideology. World War II was a fight against racism. That's what Nazism represented above all. It represented a state-enforced system of racial eugenics. The notion that inferior biological races had to be purged in order to advance everybody else. The final solution was very similar to lynchings in the South. We fought the fight against that ideology, but we fought it with a segregated military. We fought it with soldiers from the South who were part of the very value system that we said we were fighting against.

That war created a kind of a crisis in American culture. Soon after the war, Gunnar Myrdahl wrote *An American Dilemma*, which was entirely concerned with our moral schizophrenia—our stand for a whole set of values abroad that we deny at home. It was the same sort of distinction, same sort of tension between people in the eighteenth century. People who fought against the British for their rights, who said that the Stamp Act was an act of slavery but who tolerated slavery, lived with the same schizophrenia. That strain has been with us throughout, and it is still with us, in my view, and one of the reasons we still find things so difficult.

After World War II, however, the war and the rhetoric of the war began to produce some changes. Everybody dates the seminal event differently. Most people tie change to 1954, to the Supreme Court decision that declared school segregation unconstitutional and swept away the legal rationale for Jim Crow laws in the South.

I date the beginning of change from 1947, when Jackie Robinson broke the color line in baseball, because I have always believed that changes enacted on the cultural stage are more profound than those occurring on the legal stage. I was nine years old. I lived in Brooklyn and acted out that whole drama. I went to Ebbets Field. One day Ebbets Field was all white and the next day it was integrated. As a nine-year-old, I suddenly found myself sitting beside a fifty-two-year-old black guy drinking a beer and smoking a cigarette, and slapping hands with him when something good happened for the Dodgers; we were part of the drama that was going on down on the field. Everybody knew what was going on. Everybody identified with it. For this to be happening on national television as part of the mass culture that hundreds of thousands of people participated in was a drama that far exceeded in impact the business that goes on in Congress and the Supreme Court. I cannot tell you how many times I speak to audiences about cases that they have never heard about. But everybody participates in major cultural events.

Seven years after Robinson broke the color line Brown against Board of Education was decided; a couple of years after that Rosa Parks sat down on that bus in Montgomery, and we were off and running into a civil rights movement that extended civil rights for the first time since Reconstruction. That was the period in which I grew up. In 1957, when the Montgomery bus boycott occurred, and an unknown Baptist minister named Martin Luther King, Jr., emerged to lead it, I was nineteen years old. Many of us believed that Jim Crow laws were the most fundamental denial of rights that existed in the country, and remedying what happened in the South was the major social justice cause of our lives. The issue of race dominated in its size and in its importance and in its denial, as the greatest inhumane injustice that was present in the land, even though we were living in the shadow of McCarthyism, when dissent was converted into disloyalty and free speech was enormously in danger.

And we thought we could fix it. We were going to march on Washington, and we did. We were going to demand an end to Jim Crow.

We were going to demand civil rights laws that prohibited discrimination in employment or housing on the basis of race. We were going to demand a law that prohibited discrimination on the basis of race in public accommodations: privately owned places like restaurants and hotels and ballparks and theaters in which the public was expected to have access. This was radical stuff in the 1950s and the 1960s. The march on Washington took place on August 28, 1963. Barely thirty years ago.

This country is now over two hundred years old and the promise of equal rights hadn't started being addressed until thirty years ago. Back then everybody was worried about how radical we were. But the radical goals, the goals that people had as their wish list, the things that nobody thought were going to happen without a lot more bloodshed, are now the laws that college students have simply grown up with. Laws prohibiting discrimination in employment and education and housing and in public places.

By 1968, only five years after the march on Washington, we had, somewhat miraculously, gotten all those laws passed. It was really nothing less than a legal revolution. We had swept away Jim Crow. We had outlawed the very kind of legal discrimination that before had been sanctioned by law. And we had gotten rid of the segregation now, segregation tomorrow, segregation forever.

We had enforced it with troops. We had put in place a comprehensive legal mechanism to eradicate discrimination in the private as well as the public sector. And now the task was simply to enforce it through lawsuits, which we all set about busily and merrily doing . . . and with an enormous amount of success. Voting rights were enhanced. Blacks began to be elected again to state legislatures and to Congress. Thousands and thousands of black officials have been elected in the last twenty years, most of them for the first time since Reconstruction. The political system looked like it was beginning to change.

We all believed, we really believed, that by 1994, if you were to pick a year at random, that the problems of racial discrimination would have been reduced to very tiny proportions. We believed that once you got rid of Jim Crow laws, once you put in place all those laws that prohibited discrimination, everything else would automatically flow. We believed that this legal mechanism, this legal revolution would usher in the kind of colorblind society that we thought the Constitution and the Bill of Rights contemplated. That skin color would become, what my mother once told me it was when I was a little boy, just like eye color or hair color. Simply a difference. Not a difference that was related to whether or not you had an equal right to anything in life.

But it didn't turn out that way. We were all, as it turns out, extremely naive about the capacity of a legal revolution to create a political and cultural revolution, particularly in light of the history that I've described. That there was too much momentum; it was too embedded in the bones and blood of the body politic. It was too much in the heads of too many parents raising too many children to have gone away simply because laws were passed. That that is not the way the world works.

And so what happened is the laws all did get enforced, and progress has been made, and you now can see black actors in movies and black anchormen and -women in news shows. What it did is it broke down legal barriers and it allowed those people who were equipped to pass through to pass through. But it turned out that after nearly two hundred years of all that slavery and subjugation and subordination and destruction, redemption was not that easy. It turned out that those things were much more damaging, to blacks and whites alike, than anyone had imagined. And simply declaring, after those hundreds of years, that everything was now okay, didn't make it okay. The people were, in a very real sense, crippled by those two hundred years. Distorted, deformed by those two hundred years. Lyndon Johnson turned his attention to Vietnam entirely; he made a speech at Howard University. It was as if, Johnson said, you had kept somebody in chains since they were three years old and had then suddenly taken the chains off when they were thirty-five and expected that they could run

the race as fast as someone who had trained for the race and been nurtured to run, who had been fed well and had been practicing all these
years with good equipment. How could they be expected to run a race
on equal terms? Johnson suggested that something more was required, some other kind of compensation. Something like a Marshall
Plan. Something like what we did after the war with Germany and
Japan, when we poured enormous reconstructive resources into these
countries, because we knew you couldn't just walk away from that destruction and assume everything was going to rebuild itself automatically. But on race that is exactly what we did. We turned away from
those reconstructive programs; we turned away from discussing them.

Daniel Patrick Moynihan reached a point in the early 1970s in
which he began to say that the problem of race in this country might
benefit most from benign neglect. Let's just cool it. We've made a lot
of progress. Let's just step back, we're getting too hot. That was a signal for everyone to walk away. So twenty-five years of failing to address the problem was allowed to just pass.

During that time we discovered that poverty is not distributed ran-
domly. A disproportionate number of the poor were black. A disproportionate number of kids who were born poor were black. The
pathologies that our politics and subjugation created did not allow
people to just spring back to life any more than a plant that you'd neglected for years and suddenly decided to water would flourish. It
doesn't happen with plants, and didn't happen with people.

The problem of poverty is embedded in the racial problem, but
pretty soon people were saying, Wait a minute, this isn't discrimination, everybody has a right to a job. Everyone has a right to an education. If they can't make it, there must be something wrong with them.
And pretty soon we were back to the same kind of mentality that
carved blacks out of humanity and justified slavery. What was it but
that same original sin coming back and saying, Wait a minute. We
gave them all this equality. We did all this. We had the civil rights revolution. And it still isn't happening. Why is that?

One of the reasons is that nobody addressed the residual problems that I've been describing. So twenty-five years later here's the situation: You have 50 percent of black kids born into poverty. You have a situation [in which] where you live and how well you live and what school you go to and what kind of education you get and whether you have a job and what kind of a job you have still correlates more with skin color—and poverty now—than anything else. And a lot of the segregation that was broken was broken only for those people with the resources to get out. This left places like central Harlem much worse off, because now the achievers and the people who were making money and had jobs, few as they were, moved out. Because breaking down the Jim Crow laws allowed the few to escape, and left the rest imprisoned.

The prison was made worse by things like exclusionary zoning in which people from the inner cities were able to leave to the suburbs where they had zoning laws—this is true in virtually every city in the country, and it was obvious in 1968 when the Kerner Commission said that we were in danger as a result of these kinds of laws of building two Americas—one white and affluent, one black and poor. In 1968, no one paid attention—we have zoning laws which say, You can only build a house here if you have two-acre lots. You can only build a house here if it's a minimum of two bedrooms. You can only build a house here if it's a single-family dwelling; you can't have multifamily dwellings. You can't have integrated housing if you create economic criteria in the face of this situation, where the racism of two hundred years has skewed the economic distribution. So race was converted into a problem of economic stratification. Then economic laws replaced racial laws to create the same segregation that the racial laws once did, and everybody was able to say, This is not about race. This is about wanting to zone—anybody can move here. But "anybody" couldn't.

The same thing happened when factories began to relocate to the suburbs to be where their workers were. So the jobs followed into the suburbs, and people were not able to follow those jobs if they couldn't afford to live there. Then the Reagan years resulted in an abandonment of federal responsibility for funding things like education and social services at the local level. They shifted more and more responsibility to the states and cities, which had to do it out of local tax bases. The local tax bases of the suburbs were able to afford services; the local tax bases of the cities were nonexistent. So services that were desperately and disproportionately needed by the poor and mostly nonwhite and the central cities got starved and services were supplied because of a better tax base in suburbs, which were largely white. Schools were a leading example of that, but it also turned out to be true for hospitals and medical care and a whole range of other social services.

The divisions between whites and blacks continue to broaden in nearly every area—health care, employment, education. Now, fewer than 20 percent of young black men are in college, but 25 percent of black men ages eighteen to twenty-five are in prison or on parole. More people under the jurisdiction of the criminal justice system than in college. Homicide is the leading cause of death among young black men between the ages of eighteen and twenty-five. Even AIDS is rising faster in the black poor population because of intravenous drug problems.

But this is a country that prohibits the use of clean needles because of its moral fervor over the drug problem. In the Netherlands, where drug abuse is seen as a problem of health, not of crime, the way alcoholism is viewed in this country, the government gives out clean needles to drug addicts. And consequently the transmission of AIDS through intravenous use of drugs is about 6 to 8 percent in the Netherlands. In Liverpool, England, where they do the same thing, it's less than one percent. In the United States, it's 26 percent, and in New York City, it's 60 percent. When you try to propose clean needles they attack you for being part of the drug culture. But maintaining the laws which prohibit clean needles in the context of intravenous drug use and the threat of AIDS is a genocidal law. There's no other word to describe it. It's not because they don't know the facts. But this is a country that is so worked up about the morality of using drugs that it manages to ignore the morality of killing a large segment of its own population.

Drug prohibition is also the main reason why the jails are so filled. We have reached new heights—we are now the second in the world, only to the former Soviet Union, in terms of how many people per 100,000 people we imprison. There are a million and a half in prison or local jails today. Up from 200,000 or 300,000 in 1980. Do you feel safer? Is the drug problem worse? Is there more or less violence? Has building all these prisons and arresting everybody made any difference? If it has, why are they running around passing three strikes and you're out, and adding forty-six death penalties, and running all their political campaigns as if crime and violence is the number one problem? It hasn't worked.

Virtually the entire increase in arrests is drug-related. I'm not talking about violence, in which people are under the influence of drugs and commit murder or rob somebody. I'm talking about possession and sale. Most of the increase in the federal and state prisons in the last fifteen years is because of drugs; it's not because more people are getting convicted for robbery or rape or assault or burglary or homicide. It's drug-related arrests; the same kind of thing that happened during alcohol prohibition. And 65 to 70 percent of the people in those prisons are black or Hispanic.

According to government studies, 12 percent of blacks in this country are using or selling drugs. But 38 to 40 percent of all drug-related arrests are blacks. Why is that? If you tell people that most of the prisons are filling up with blacks on drug-related cases, they will tell you that that's because they're the ones who are doing the crime. But it isn't so. They're the ones who are getting arrested for doing the crime. It's not because the cops are racist. It's harder than that. It's because when you're poor you do the crime out on the street where people can see you. And when you're affluent you do the crime behind closed doors where the cops don't see you.

Think of who gets arrested for prostitution in this country. It isn't the fancy call girls, it's the street prostitutes. And the street prostitutes are mostly women of color, and the fancy call girls are mostly white. You can turn on cable television in any city in this country and dial a phone number and get a girl delivered to your apartment and use your credit card. That's all against the law. Nobody ever arrests those people. But when [New York's mayor] Rudolph Giuliani wants to improve the quality of life, he sends cops into the mean streets of Bedford-Stuyvesant and central Harlem and he sweeps the streets of all these eyesores and he picks up all the prostitutes. The ones he picks up are not the only ones doing it; they're just the easiest to see and arrest. The same thing is true for drugs. When cocaine use was rampant on college campuses in the seventies, rampant in Wall Street brokerage houses, rampant in Hollywood, none of those folks got arrested. They were arresting the people on the stoops and the streets and the alleys. The drug business is an enormous enterprise—you know Al Capone didn't kill people because he was drunk—and most folks who are shooting people now are not high on cocaine, they're trafficking in cocaine. They're settling commercial disputes with their customers and competitors with Uzis instead of lawyers. If you're Shenley's and Seagrams and you have a price war, you get an advertising agency or hire a lawyer. But if you're a drug dealer on 125th Street and you're having a price war or a dispute with a customer who hasn't paid, you can't use the legal system because they have defined you out of it. That's what prohibition is. So you settle it with force. And that's one of the reasons why we've had this enormous spread of guns, fueled by drug profits. That's one of the reasons why public housing in the inner cities is a war zone. That's one of the reasons why five-year-old kids go to school today having seen kids their own age shot not once, not twice, but three or four or five times. And we are told by senators like Paul Simon in Illinois, otherwise a liberal, that the way to stop those kids from being violent is to ban them from watching Arnold Schwarzenegger movies. Go after TV violence. Let's stop *Murder, She Wrote* from being on in prime time. Janet Reno actually said that.

My wife is a kindergarten teacher in midtown New York. She has a little girl who comes in who's five years old whose mother is nineteen. The mother sometimes brings her to school—if she brings her at all— late, and in her underwear. There's no man in sight. The mother is spaced out on something. This kid has seen kids her age shot and killed. She's five years old. Bullets are a way of life. There were thirty-five kids killed in one year recently in New York, just from bystander shootings, just from bullets flying. And we are told by the people we elect to solve our problems that the way to stop this kid from being violent is to censor television violence. My kid could watch Arnold Schwarzenegger in movies all day long and he will not go out and shoot anybody. Why is that? But the politicians don't want to address these problems. They don't want to address the poverty. They don't want to address the economic problems. They don't want to address the drug problem. What they want to do is get elected. So they pass laws that appear to be tough on crime without being tough. They pass laws to build more prisons when that isn't working. They will never pass a law to address the underlying problem, which is meanwhile getting worse.

The enormous increase in technology in the last fifteen or twenty years, the conversion to a high-tech economy, is creating a problem that is a little bit like what happened in England in the Industrial Revolution in the early nineteenth century, where the handweavers were replaced by the power loom. And while technical changes like that ultimately lift the living standards of everybody, ultimately means never for the people of the generation in which the technological change came.

So the weavers in England during the Industrial Revolution were out of a job. They were out of a life. They began getting angry. They tried to organize to get the government to do something about it. The government didn't do anything about it, so they became Luddites. They went into the factories and tried to smash the power looms. They became the subject of criminal action and pretty soon they were broken and began to flood the cities. The situation in the cities in England was well described by Charles Dickens novels. Kids without parents flooded the streets. Crime went up. But it was just disorder crime. Petty thievery. Survival crime. A whole set of people were shut out of the economy. Calls for incarcerative solutions went up. The English poor laws came out of that history. Put them in orphanages they said then, just as Newt Gingrich says now. Put them in work-houses, they said then. Put them on Workfair, we say today. Don't just give them money because they've been victimized by a technological change. Punish them because they don't want to work. How do you know they don't want to work if you haven't supplied them with jobs? No matter, make them work at menial jobs beneath going wages. Make them work off their welfare or else cut them off welfare.

During the Industrial Revolution in England, the people who were in a position to benefit from it, those who had capital, got very wealthy. But all the other people, the handweavers and their families, were shut out of the economy entirely, so you had an enormous wage disparity. Progress overall looked okay. But beneath the overall there were these wide differences that were a social disaster. And the social disaster was met with repression, as I think it is being met today.

Average is a funny thing, you know. It's like the old statistician's story about the guy who stands on one foot on a hot stove and one foot on a cake of dry ice and is described as being on the average comfortable. Never read a statistic in the newspaper without remembering that, because you will read that the economy is doing well. Productivity is up, inflation is down, unemployment is down—the economy, the Gross National Product, all these measures that they use. But meanwhile, what's happening now is the same thing that happened in England in the nineteenth century. People who are in a position—this time it's not so much capital as it is people with skills and education—if you're in the position to know how to work microprocessors or invent them or develop them . . . if you're in a position to know how to run a complicated piece of machinery based on computer technology, you're doing real well, or you can do well. But if you don't have those skills, you are shut out entirely. There has been a more dramatic wage disparity in the last twenty years than at any time in this century.

When this kind of economic crisis is superimposed on the racial conditions of this country, everybody runs from it. No politician is willing to talk about these problems, no political campaign addresses these problems. No one will debate such things in Congress. The greatest leap that the liberals made in the crime bill, in terms of prevention, was to create midnight basketball leagues. Hey, I'm all in favor of midnight basketball leagues, but the notion that that is what is going to cure the problems that we face in our inner cities is so bizarrely irresponsible that it is hard to know how to react to it. But these are the people who say they're being tough on crime. All that they're accomplishing with their incarcerative, punitive response is identifying scapegoats. That's what's going on in California with proposition 187. Now, despite all our progress, the original sin is beginning to seep back because blacks are still at the lower end in education, in employment, in IQ testing. What can it be? If it isn't us, you see, it must be them.

And so suddenly Charles Murray writes *The Bell Curve* and he discovers that it really is, after all, genetic. It has to be genetic or else we could not live with ourselves. It's no different than the people who justified slavery by convincing themselves that blacks weren't human. That blacks weren't human or else we couldn't have Jim Crow laws. Now it's genetic. It has nothing to do with the climate we created in which the seeds were planted.

I saw a study two days ago which said that twice as many blacks give birth to low-birth-weight babies as whites. Environment doesn't just mean whether the sun comes out, or whether there's a nice house to grow up in with two parents. Environment includes what happens right after conception, what happens in the prenatal environment. If 50 percent of black kids are born poor; if black mothers are the ones who are not getting prenatal care and good nutrition; if they're often living in situations in which they're getting beat up by guys that they're with; if there aren't any social programs that deal with that problem . . . what is the environment in which that fetus is growing? What is it that is producing—is it the genes? If you took tropical plants and planted them in Minnesota in December they wouldn't grow, and you'd be a fool to blame it on the seeds.

But Charles Murray is here. As a scientific study it is total fraud. It repeats pseudoscientific findings that have been discredited many times. The last time this business arose big time was the last time you had Eastern European immigrants. In those times the Jews were feebleminded. Now the Jews are smart. I was tempted to write a letter to Murray. He has something in his book that says that Ashkenazi Jews of Eastern European origin are at the top of IQ scores. I was going to write a letter to the *Times* saying that, as an Ashkenazi Jew of Eastern European origin, and the inheritor of a richer intellectual endowment than Murray, I am here to tell him he is a real slow learner. But it's worse than that. It's that this guy is promoting himself through a discredited theory as if it were science because he and his publishers and his movement know a good audience when they see one. We are at a time when the country is once again ready to believe, because it cannot accept or talk about the alternative—to believe that it is about them, it is not about us, it is about genes, it is not about our history.

But it *is* about our history. And I think that if we do not begin to talk about this candidly—as difficult as that is to do—and if we do not find a way to create a constituency for change, we will never hear it on the political agenda. It will never be talked about in Congress until it's talked about in places like this all across the country, in far larger numbers and far more candidly than we are now doing. Race is not a popular subject these days. It has to be talked about not because, as John has written, talking about it is self-executing, it is a daunting problem to figure out how to turn this system around before we usher in some very dark and punitive days, which I think we are really on the edge of. This is a political culture which is lurching to the right and being whipped up into a frenzy by self-promoters like Rush Limbaugh, and which is being pandered to by everyone in the political system, including most of the liberal Democrats who are afraid to stand up to it and tell you that if you lobby in Washington all the time. This is a political system which passed the crime bill that won't make us safer, doesn't control crime, and doesn't address the underlying social problems. The same crime bill that was defeated in the Reagan and Bush [administrations] was passed this time because in the Reagan and Bush [administrations] the liberal Democrats opposed it because it was Reagan. Now it's their guy in the White House, and they believed that if they didn't pass they couldn't win the midterm elections. So they passed the bill and they're still not going to win the midterm elections. And they're going to make the problem worse. Until we have generated enough of a constituency of morality in this country that is willing to talk about these problems and begin pressing them upon our politicians, they will not be on the political agenda. But first, we must put them on our agenda.

OCTOBER 1994

audre lorde

audre lorde

Audre Lorde was born in New York City in 1934 and died of cancer in Saint Croix, the Virgin Islands, in 1992. She was a poet and essayist who worked as a librarian and creative writing professor. Her books include *Zani: A New Spelling of My Name, Use of the Erotic: The Erotic as Power, The Cancer Journals, Sister Outsider*, and *The Marvelous Arithmetics of Distance*, which was nominated for a National Book Critics Circle Award in poetry.

A powerful writer and speaker, Lorde articulated with a passionate anger the reality of being a woman of color in America, and made clear the relationship between racism and sexism. She was an inspirational individual and social leader who wrote important essays on lesbian mothering, the erotic, and surviving cancer.

In *The Cancer Journals* she wrote: "What is there possibly left for us to be afraid of, after we have dealt face to face with death, and not embraced it? Once I accept the existence of dying as a life process, who can ever have power over me again?"

The following speech was given as a keynote presentation at a Women's Studies Conference at the University of Connecticut in 1981.

the uses of anger: women responding to racism

Racism: The belief in the inherent superiority of one race over all others and thereby the right to dominance, manifest and implied.

Women respond to racism. My response to racism is anger. I have lived with that anger, ignoring it, feeding upon it, learning to use it before it laid my visions to waste, for most of my life. Once I did it in silence, afraid of the weight. My fear of anger taught me nothing. Your fear of that anger will teach you nothing, also.

Women responding to racism means women responding to anger—the anger of exclusion, of unquestioned privilege, of racial distortions, of silence, ill-use, stereotyping, defensiveness, misnaming, betrayal, and cooptation.

My anger is a response to racists' attitudes and to the actions and presumptions that arise out of those attitudes. If your dealings with other women reflect those attitudes, then my anger and your attendant fears are spotlights that can be used for growth in the same way I have used learning to express anger for my growth. But for corrective surgery, not guilt. Guilt and defensiveness are bricks in a wall against which we all flounder; they serve none of our futures.

Because I do not want this to become a theoretical discussion, I am going to give a few examples of interchanges between women that illustrate these points. In the interest of time, I am going to cut them short. I want you to know there were many more.

For example:

- I speak out of direct and particular anger at an academic conference, and a white woman says, "Tell me how you feel but don't say it too harshly or I cannot hear you." But is it my manner that keeps her from hearing, or the threat of a message that her life may change?

- The Women's Studies Program of a southern university invites a Black woman to read following a weeklong forum on Black and white women. "What has this week given to you?" I ask. The most vocal white woman says, "I think I've gotten a lot, I feel Black women really understand me a lot better now; they have a better idea of where I'm coming from." As if understanding her lay at the core of the racist problem.

- After fifteen years of a women's movement which professes to address the life concerns and possible futures of all women, I still hear, on campus after campus, "How can we address the issues of racism? No women of Color attended." Or, the other side of that statement, "We have no one in our department equipped to teach their work." In other words, racism is a Black women's problem, a problem of women of Color, and only we can discuss it.

- After I read from my work entitled "Poems for Women in Rage," a white woman asks me: "Are you going to do anything with how we can deal directly with *our* anger? I feel it's so important." I ask, "How do you use *your* rage?" And then I have to turn away from the blank look in her eyes, before she can invite me to participate in her own annihilation. I do not exist to feel her anger for her.

- White women are beginning to examine their relationships to Black women, yet often I hear them wanting only to deal with little colored children across the roads of childhood, the beloved nursemaid, the occasional second-grade classmate—those tender memories of what was once mysterious and intriguing or neutral. You avoid the childhood assumptions formed by the raucous laughter at Rastus and Alfalfa, the acute message of your mommy's handkerchief spread on the park bench because I had just been sitting there, the indelible and dehumanizing portraits of Amos 'n Andy and your daddy's humorous bedtime stories.

- I wheel my two-year-old daughter in a shopping cart through a supermarket in Eastchester in 1967, and a little white girl riding past in her mother's cart calls out excitedly, "Oh look, Mommy, a baby maid!" And your mother shushes you, but she does not correct you. And so fifteen years later, at a conference on racism, you can still find that story humorous. But I hear your laughter is full of terror and dis-ease.

- A white academic welcomes the appearance of a collection by non-Black women of Color. "It allows me to deal with racism without dealing with the harshness of Black women," she says to me.

- At an international cultural gathering of women, a well-known white American woman poet interrupts the reading of the work of women of Color to read her own poem, and then dashes off to an "important panel."

If women in the academy truly want a dialogue about racism, it will require recognizing the needs and the living contexts of other women. When an academic woman says, "I can't afford it," she may mean she is making a choice about how to spend her available money. But when a woman on welfare says, "I can't afford it," she means she is surviving on an amount of money that was barely subsistence in 1972, and she often does not have enough to eat. Yet the National Women's Studies Association here in 1981 holds a conference in which it commits itself to responding to racism, yet refuses to waive the registration fee for poor women and women of Color who wished to present and conduct workshops. This has made it impossible for many women of Color—for instance, Wilmette Brown, of Black Women for Wage for Housework—to participate in this conference. Is this to be merely another case of the academy discussing life within the closed circuits of the academy?

To the white women present who recognize these attitudes as familiar, but most of all, to all my sisters of Color who live and survive thousands of such encounters—to my sisters of Color who like me still tremble their rage under harness, or who sometimes question the expression of our rage as useless and disruptive (the two most popular accusations)—I want to speak about anger, my anger, and what I have learned from my travels through its dominions.

Everything can be used / except what is wasteful / (you will / need to re-member this when you are accused of destruction.) (From "For Each of You," first published in *From a Land Where Other People Live* [Detroit: Broadside Press, 1973], and collected in *Chosen Poems: Old and New*, p. 42.)

Every woman has a well-stocked arsenal of anger potentially useful against those oppressions, personal and institutional, which brought that anger into being. Focused with precision it can become a power-ful source of energy serving progress and change. And when I speak of change, I do not mean a simple switch of positions or a temporary lessening of tensions, nor the ability to smile or feel good. I am speak-ing of a basic and radical alteration in those assumptions underlining our lives.

I have seen situations where white women hear a racist remark, re-sent what has been said, become filled with fury, and remain silent be-cause they are afraid. That unexpressed anger lies within them like an undetonated device, usually to be hurled at the first woman of Color who talks about racism.

But anger expressed and translated into action in the service of our vision and our future is a liberating and strengthening act of clarifica-tion, for it is in the painful process of this translation that we identify who are our allies with whom we have grave differences, and who are our genuine enemies.

Anger is loaded with information and energy. When I speak of women of Color, I do not only mean Black women. The woman of Color who is not Black and who charges me with rendering her invis-ible by assuming that her struggles with racism are identical with mine has something to tell me that I had better learn from, lest we both waste ourselves fighting the truths between us. If I participate, knowingly or otherwise, in my sister's oppression and she calls me on it, to answer her anger with my own only blankets the substance of our exchange with reaction. It wastes energy. And yes, it is very difficult to stand still and to listen to another woman's voice delineate an agony I do not share, or one to which I myself have contributed.

In this place we speak removed from the more blatant reminders of our embattlement as women. This need not blind us to the size and complexities of the forces mounting against us and all that is most human within our environment. We are not here as women examining racism in a political and social vacuum. We operate in the teeth of a system for which racism and sexism are primary, established, and necessary props of profit. Women responding to racism is a topic so dangerous that when the local media attempt to discredit this conference they choose to focus upon the provision of lesbian housing as a diversionary device—as if the Hartford *Courant* dare not mention the topic chosen for discussion here, racism, lest it become apparent that women are in fact attempting to examine and to alter all the repressive conditions of our lives.

Mainstream communication does not want women, particularly white women, responding to racism. It wants racism to be accepted as an immutable given in the fabric of your existence like eveningtime or the common cold.

So we are working in a context of opposition and threat, the cause of which is certainly not the angers which lie between us, but rather that virulent hatred leveled against all women, people of Color, lesbians and gay men, poor people—against all of us who are seeking to examine the particulars of our lives as we resist our oppressions, moving toward coalition and effective action.

Any discussion among women about racism must include the recognition and the use of anger. This discussion must be direct and creative because it is crucial. We cannot allow our fear of anger to deflect us nor seduce us into settling for anything less than the hard work of excavating honesty; we must be quite serious about the choice of this topic and the angers entwined within it, because, rest assured, our opponents are quite serious about their hatred of us and of what we are trying to do here.

And while we scrutinize the often painful face of each other's anger, please remember that it is not our anger which makes me caution you to lock your doors at night and not to wander the streets of Hartford alone. It is the hatred which lurks in those streets, that urge to destroy us all if we truly work for change rather than merely indulge in academic rhetoric.

This hatred and our anger are very different. Hatred is the fury of those who do not share our goals, and its object is death and destruction. Anger is a grief of distortions between peers, and its object is change. But our time is getting shorter. We have been raised to view any difference other than sex as a reason for destruction, and for Black women and white women to face each other's angers without denial or immobility or silence or guilt is in itself a heretical and generative idea. It implies peers meeting upon a common basis to examine difference, and to alter those distortions which history has created around our difference. For it is those distortions which separate us. And we must ask ourselves: Who profits from all this?

Women of Color in America have grown up within a symphony of anger, at being silenced, at being unchosen, at knowing that when we survive, it is in spite of a world that takes for granted our lack of humanness, and which hates our very existence outside of its service. And I say *symphony* rather than *cacophony* because we have had to learn to orchestrate those furies so that they do not tear us apart. We have had to learn to move through them and use them for strength and force and insight within our daily lives. Those of us who did not learn this difficult lesson did not survive. And part of my anger is always libation for my fallen sisters.

Anger is an appropriate reaction to racist attitudes, as is fury when the actions arising from those attitudes do not change. To those women here who fear the anger of women of Color more than they own unscrutinized racist attitudes, I ask: Is the anger of women of

Color more threatening than the woman-hatred that tinges all aspects of our lives?

It is not the anger of other women that will destroy us but our refusals to stand still, to listen to its rhythms, to learn within it, to move beyond the manner of presentation to the substance, to tap that anger as an important source of empowerment.

I cannot hide my anger to spare you guilt, nor hurt feelings, nor answering anger; for to do so insults and trivializes all our efforts. Guilt is not a response to anger; it is a response to one's own actions or lack of action. If it leads to change then it can be useful, since it is then no longer guilt but the beginning of knowledge. Yet all too often, guilt is just another name for impotence, for defensiveness destructive of communication; it becomes a device to protect ignorance and the continuation of things the way they are, the ultimate protection for changelessness.

Most women have not developed tools for facing anger constructively. CR groups in the past, largely white, dealt with how to express anger, usually at the world of men. And these groups were made up of white women who shared the terms of their oppressions. There was usually little attempt to articulate the genuine differences between women, such as those of race, color, age, class, and sexual identity. There was no apparent need at that time to examine the contradictions of self, woman as oppressor. There was work on expressing anger, but very little on anger directed against each other. No tools were developed to deal with other women's anger except to avoid it, deflect it, or flee from it under a blanket of guilt.

I have no creative use for guilt, yours or my own. Guilt is only another way of avoiding informed action, of buying time out of the pressing need to make clear choices, out of the approaching storm that can feed the earth as well as bend the trees. If I speak to you in anger, at least I have spoken to you: I have not put a gun to your head and shot you down in the street; I have not looked at your bleeding sister's body and asked, "What did she do to deserve it?" This was the reaction of two white women to Mary Church Terrell's telling of the lynching of a pregnant Black woman whose baby was then torn from her body. That was in 1921, and Alice Paul had just refused to publicly endorse the enforcement of the Nineteenth Amendment for all women—by refusing to endorse the inclusion of women of Color, although we had worked to help bring about that amendment.

The angers between women will not kill us if we can articulate them with precision, if we listen to the content of what is said with at least as much intensity as we defend ourselves against the manner of saying. When we turn from anger we turn from insight, saying we will accept only the designs already known, deadly and safely familiar. I have tried to learn my anger's usefulness to me, as well as its limitations.

For women raised to fear, too often anger threatens annihilation. In the male construct of brute force, we were taught that our lives depended upon the goodwill of patriarchal power. The anger of others was to be avoided at all costs because there was nothing to be learned from it but pain, a judgment that we had been bad girls, come up lacking, not done what we were supposed to do. And if we accept our powerlessness, then of course any anger can destroy us.

But the strength of women lies in recognizing differences between us as creative, and in standing to those distortions which we inherited without blame but which are now ours to alter. The angers of women can transform difference through insight into power. For anger between peers births change, not destruction, and the discomfort and sense of loss it often causes is not fatal but a sign of growth.

My response to racism is anger. That anger has eaten clefts into my living only when it remained unspoken, useless to anyone. It has also served me in classrooms without light or learning, where the work and history of Black women was less than a vapor. It has served me as fire in the ice zone of uncomprehending eyes of white women who see in my experience and the experience of my people only new reasons for fear or guilt. And my anger is no excuse for not dealing with your blindness, no reason to withdraw from the results of your own actions.

When women of Color speak out of the anger that laces so many of our contacts with white women, we are often told that we are "creating a mood of hopelessness," "preventing white women from getting past guilt," or "standing in the way of trusting communication and action." All these quotes come directly from letters to me from members of this organization within the last two years. One woman wrote, "Because you are Black and Lesbian, you seem to speak with the moral authority of suffering." Yes, I am Black and lesbian, and what you hear in my voice is fury, not suffering. Anger, not moral authority. There is a difference.

To turn aside from the anger of Black women with excuses or the pretexts of intimidation is to award no one power—it is merely another way of preserving racial blindness, the power of unaddressed privilege, unbreached, intact. Guilt is only another form of objectification. Oppressed peoples are always being asked to stretch a little more, to bridge the gap between blindness and humanity. Black women are expected to use our anger only in the service of other people's salvation or learning. But that time is over. My anger has meant pain to me but it has also meant survival, and before I give it up I'm going to be sure that there is something at least as powerful to replace it on the road to clarity.

What woman here is so enamored of her own oppression that she cannot see her heelprint upon another woman's face? What woman's terms of oppression have become precious and necessary to her as a ticket into the fold of the righteous, away from the cold winds of self-scrutiny?

I am a lesbian woman of Color whose children eat regularly because I work in a university. If their full bellies make me fail to recognize my commonality with a woman of Color whose children do not eat because she cannot find work, or who has no children because her insides are rotted from home abortions and sterilization; if I fail to recognize the lesbian who chooses not to have children, the woman who remains closeted because homophobic communities are her only life support, the woman who chooses silence instead of another death, the woman who is terrified lest my anger trigger the explosion of hers; if I fail to recognize them as other faces of myself, then I am contributing not only to each of their oppressions but also to my own, and the anger which stands between us then must be used for clarity and mutual empowerment, not for evasion by guilt or for further separation. I am not free while any woman is unfree, even when her shackles are very different from my own. And I am not free as long as one person of Color remains chained. Nor is any one of you.

I speak here as a woman of Color who is not bent upon destruction, but upon survival. No woman is responsible for altering the psyche of her oppressor, even when that psyche is embodied in another woman. I have suckled the wolf's lip of anger and I have used it for illumination, laughter, protection, fire in places where there was no light, no food, no sisters, no quarter. We are not goddesses or matriarchs or edifices of divine forgiveness; we are not fiery fingers of judgment or instruments of flagellation; we are women forced back always upon our woman's power. We have learned to use anger as we have learned to use the dead flesh of animals, and bruised, battered, and changing, we have survived and grown and, in Angela Wilson's words, we *are* moving on. With or without uncolored women. We use whatever strengths we have fought for, including anger, to help define and fashion a world where all our sisters can grow, where our children can love, and where the power of touching and meeting another woman's difference and wonder will eventually transcend the need for destruction.

For it is not the anger of Black women which is dripping down over this globe like a diseased liquid. It is not my anger that launches rockets, spends over sixty thousand dollars a second on missiles and other agents of war and death, slaughters children in cities, stockpiles nerve gas and chemical bombs, sodomized our daughters and our earth. It is not the anger of Black women which corrodes into blind, dehumanizing power, bent upon the annihilation of us all unless we meet it with what we have, our power to examine and to redefine the terms upon which we will live and work; our power to envision and to reconstruct, anger by painful anger, stone upon heavy stone, a future of pollinating difference and the earth to support our choices.

We welcome all women who can meet us, face-to-face, beyond objectification and beyond guilt.

john powell

john powell

John powell is professor of law at the University of Minnesota Law School, and executive director of the Institute on Race and Poverty. He received his B.A. from Stanford University, and his J.D. from the University of California, Berkeley.

Prior to joining the faculty of the University of Minnesota Law School, powell served as National Legal Director of the American Civil Liberties Union. He has taught law at Columbia University, Harvard University, the University of Miami, and the University of San Francisco.

A nationally recognized authority on issues relating to race/poverty and the law, powell is an imaginative thinker and speaker, with a tremendous ability to explain in human terms how complex laws and policies affect our daily lives.

are you going on the march?

It is a few weeks before the Million Man March, and a number of my closest friends come to Minneapolis to participate in an advisory board meeting of the Institute on Race and Poverty, which I direct. At an Indian restaurant one night we get to talking about the upcoming march. There are seven of us at dinner, all African-Americans, friends that I love and respect, who deeply influence my thinking. I know the three men from law school at Stanford, and I used to work closely with Maya, the only woman in the group, at the ACLU in New York. John Calmore and I are joined by our teenage sons, who have been good friends themselves since they were young boys.

Only one of us, Roger, a partner in a San Francisco law firm, declares that he is going to the march. Roger is brimming with an uncharacteristic enthusiasm. He's excited about taking the trip with his grown son. Roger is a man who's always had a social conscience, but he is a buttoned-down partner now, who lives well and drives around the Bay Area in a snazzy Mercedes. He shares his excitement about the march and tries to persuade the rest of us to join him. "I missed Dr. King's march, I'm not going to miss this one."

The genuine reason for Roger's enthusiasm may be the opportunity the march offers for having a profound experience with his son, a young man in his early twenties who's come too close to becoming a statistic. Roger is afraid, like so many of us are, of losing his son to the blight of drugs and crime that plague African-American youth.

Lately, I've been worrying about my fifteen-year-old son, Fon. He has become uncommunicative and is not keeping up with his schoolwork. He picked up a strange habit of leaving the house wearing my clothes and shoes. I wasted a lot of time looking all over the house for my shoes. After a few weeks of this, I bought him a new pair of shoes like mine. "I don't want those shoes," he said, "I want your shoes." I keep reminding myself how important fathers are to their sons.

We are all sitting around a big table, eating hot Indian food. Fon and his friend Jonathan are engaged in an intellectual duel of their own about the origins of Fahrenheit as a concept. They are safe for now, bragging about all that they know and all that they don't know, as the larger group of us continue to interrogate each other about the march.

Maya, a tall, striking woman who works for the Justice Department, has a mouth for every kind of talk. She starts out in a pristine, intellectual tone: "How is it that we define the problems of the black community in a way that excludes women?" But as soon as she starts talking about the subservient role prescribed for black women by the Nation of Islam, she breaks into street talk. "I don't care who the motherfucker is, if he tells me to stay home and do the dishes, he can kiss my ass."

"Whoa, Maya," says Paul, the president of one of the largest black savings and loan companies in the country. He points out that it is too easy to stand back and be critical of our black leadership. He doesn't believe that we can go on addressing the issues as individuals alone.

I find myself agreeing with that assertion, as I suspect the offer made to middle-class blacks to be individuals, in the context of race, is more false than true. Am I being seen as an individual when cabs pass me in New York, or while the police question me as I fumble with a key to my front door? I fear that the individuality offered by the white community may really be an offer to pass into solidarity with the dominant white structure, in tacit opposition to other blacks.

My friend John Calmore has been uncharacteristically quiet during our discussion. A professor at Loyola University, John has always declared himself a "race man." He's never been content to simply blend in as a "man."

Having the same first name, Calmore and I have called each other by our last names for years. Once when we were debating during a forum at Harvard, we took opposing views on a particular issue and really got into it. When my turn came around I'd say, "Calmore, that's a very impressive argument you put forth, unfortunately. . . ." And Calmore, who has a magnificent voice, would spread it like honey. "On the contrary, powell, . . ." Later, a man from the audience called out a question to me. "powell" he said, and I turned to the man and said, "I'm sorry, but you can't call me powell. You don't know me. He can call me powell, because he's my friend."

"Calmore," I say, "what do you think about the march?"

"I don't have a lot of passion one way or the other, powell. I think the problem for me is Farrakhan. The man comes with substantial baggage."

"Amen," Maya says. "I don't mind that Farrakhan's called for a male-only march, it's the rest of his bullshit that pisses me off—that women need to know their place, that men have to go home and re-assert their place in the family."

Calmore smiles at me. "What are you going to do, powell?"

I shake my head and acknowledge that Minister Farrakhan's call for black men to come together for atonement, and to take responsibility for our own community, is a powerful message in this dismal racial wasteland. Even without a program or structure to sustain the energy of this message, its spiritual importance cannot be understated.

But despite a number of good things about the march, I believe it misses a tremendous opportunity to bring a deeper understanding to problems facing the black community and the country. While the concern leading up to the march focuses on black violence and the need for more positive agency within the black community, especially by black men, there is little mention of the role of the new breed of racists with their thinly veiled agenda to further segregate and disem-power the black community. What about the Republican-led Con-gress that condones racial polarization and white racial hierarchy? Why not focus, in part, on their agenda? Clearly many blacks can take more control of their destinies, but it is wrong to believe that we will be able to address our problems without dealing with racial polarization and white supremacy in all its forms. A lack of jobs, education, and hope is much of what is fueling the violence in the black community. Little discussion in advance of the march goes beyond the slogans of self-help and white racism, to speak to the structural and institutional problems facing the black community and this country.

And there is an underbelly to Minister Farrakhan's message to the sexes, which seems eerily close to the message of the Christian right and the Promise Keepers: men rule. In a community where men have been so absent and marginal in schools, jobs, and family, this message has some appeal, but it is fraught with danger. I do not buy it from the Nation of Islam any more than from the Christian right.

My friend Paul speaks up again: "Aren't you demanding too much of our leadership?"

"But what about the continued attack by the Nation on Jews?" It makes sense to me that black America would be distrustful and angry at white America. But the singling out of Jews has never made sense to me. This does not mean that there might not be differences, regarding opinions over Israel and the Palestinians, or affirmative action. But as Paul repeatedly reminds us at the restaurant, relationships cannot be based on perfect agreements. When I look around and see people like Newt Gingrich, Jesse Helms, Clarence Thomas, Pat Robertson, and Pete Wilson posing vocal and serious threats to the well-being of blacks, I do not see Jews. Indeed, Jews are often attacked by those groups.

So it is with a great pause that I resolve not to go to D.C. But it is not because of who or what is left out, but because the cost of solidarity is, for me, too high. I am worried about this country and especially about African-Americans. The country's concern about racial justice has been short-lived, and the old racism of the 1940s and 1950s has given birth to a racism that is more subtle but just as deadly for the black community and the country as a whole. Many powerful people and forces have a vested interest in racial polarity and hostility.

Even when racism assumes a faceless aspect, the human effects of, say, redlining, and poor schools in black neighborhoods, are very real. When the press cites the escalating incarceration rate for African-American males, it isn't an abstract concept to my friends and me. We talk about our sons, nephews, and friends who are in jail or who have been recently harassed by the police. We understand that the most dangerous and immediate threat to all blacks, especially young black males, is posed by other black males. Like animals trapped in crowded spaces without sufficient means to take care of our basic needs, we are both the victim and the prey.

Like many black professionals, I do not live at the center of the racial poverty trap. But escape from the reaches of racism is always incomplete. Although I do not want to live where risk of death on the streets is higher than in war, my goal is not simply to escape racism but to transform it. My worry when my son or daughter comes home late at night is different from the worries that I caused my parents. And I'm confused. How do I teach my children about the effects of racism on low-income blacks while warning them not to go after the sun goes down into the areas of the city most affected by racism?

My son and I return to the heart of the black community to get our hair cut. There is too much poverty and desperation here. But in going into the community, I also experience a sense of well-being and familiarity that is comforting. For a short period of time we are not the racial Other. Within this comfort, however, I also have a heightened sense of violence that stalks the streets and constantly threatens to take form and live. I do not experience the joy and ease that was part of my life growing up in a poor black community in Detroit. The despair and violence does not allow this community to easily be home for me or many of the people still living there.

After our haircuts, my son and I return to our house. But we know, despite the placid and aesthetic nature of this community, this is not home. Our white neighbors keep at a distance that is not explained by Minnesota reserve. And I know now that we are all too conspicuous to those charged with keeping white society safe from blacks, the police.

The threat of random violence from a black male receives the threat of racial violence from the police, and the spiritual isolation grows.

At dinner, the experience of being black in America is not the cause for much discussion. It is only too familiar. There is a vast common ground that the group at the dinner table shares. Any one of us, with slight modifications, can describe the state of racial realities in America without incurring much disagreement.

As friends, we can disagree openly, and even lovingly, about the march. And afterwards, when the rest of us hear from Roger about his experience with his son—how powerful the march was, how it made his son and him so proud to see themselves among a massive wave of beautiful black men—we cheer for him, and are cheered by his good news.

peggy mcintosh

peggy mcIntosh

Peggy McIntosh is associate director of the Wellesley College Center for Research on Women. She also directs the National S.E.E.D. Project on Inclusive Curriculum.

During her work in women's studies in the late seventies and early eighties, which involved bringing materials on women into college curricula, McIntosh discovered a corollary between male privilege and white privilege, and realized that her project needed to evolve into a multicultural enterprise. A national leader in education, McIntosh has lectured and led workshops across the country based on her personal findings on white privilege. "After frustration with men who would not recognize male privilege," she says, "I decided to try to work on myself by identifying some of the daily effects of white privilege in my life."

white privilege: unpacking the invisible knapsack

Through work to bring materials from Women's Studies into the rest of the curriculum, I have often noticed men's unwillingness to grant that they are overprivileged, even though they may grant that women are disadvantaged. They may say they will work to improve women's status, in the society, the university, or the curriculum, but they can't or won't support the idea of lessening men's. Denials which amount to taboos surround the subject of advantages which men gain from women's disadvantages. These denials protect male privilege from being fully acknowledged, lessened, or ended.

Thinking through unacknowledged male privilege as a phenomenon, I realized that since hierarchies in our society are interlocking, there was most likely a phenomenon of white privilege which was similarly denied and protected. As a white person, I realized I had been taught about racism as something which puts others at a disadvantage, but had been taught not to see one of its corollary aspects, white privilege, which puts me at an advantage.

I think whites are carefully taught not to recognize white privilege, as males are taught not to recognize male privilege. So I have begun in an untutored way to ask what it is like to have white privilege. I have come to see white privilege as an invisible package of unearned assets which I can count on cashing in on each day, but about which I was "meant" to remain oblivious. White privilege is like an invisible weightless knapsack of special provisions, maps, passports, codebooks, visas, clothes, tools, and blank checks.

Describing white privilege makes one newly accountable. As we in Women's Studies work to reveal male privilege and ask men to give up

White Privilege: Unpacking the Invisible Knapsack © *1988 by Peggy McIntosh. Permission to duplicate must be obtained from the author. Excerpting is not authorized. A longer analysis and list of privileges, including heterosexual privilege, is available for $6.00 from Peggy McIntosh, Wellesley College Center for Research on Women, Wellesley, MA 02181; (617) 283-2520; FAX (617) 283-2504.*

some of their power, so one who writes about having white privilege must ask, "Having described it, what will I do to lessen or end it?"

After I realized the extent to which men work from a base of unacknowledged privilege, I understood that much of their oppressiveness was unconscious. Then I remembered the frequent charges from women of color that white women whom they encounter are oppressive. I began to understand why we are justly seen as oppressive, even when we don't see ourselves that way. I began to count the ways in which I enjoy unearned skin privilege and have been conditioned into oblivion about its existence.

My schooling gave me no training in seeing myself as an oppressor, as an unfairly advantaged person, or as a participant in a damaged culture. I was taught to see myself as an individual whose moral state depended on her individual moral will. My schooling followed the pattern my colleague Elizabeth Minnich has pointed out: Whites are taught to think of their lives as morally neutral, normative, and average, and also ideal, so that when we work to benefit others, this is seen as work which will allow "them" to be more like "us."

I decided to try to work on myself at least by identifying some of the daily ways in which I experience white privilege in my own life situation and in my own workplace, by contrast with African-American women in the same line of work. I have chosen those conditions which I think in my case *attach somewhat more to skin-color privilege* than to class, religion, ethnic status, or geographical location, though of course all these other factors are intricately intertwined. As far as I can see, my African-American coworkers, friends, and acquaintances with whom I come into daily or frequent contact in this particular time, place, and line of work cannot count on most of these conditions.

1. I can if I wish arrange to be in the company of people of my race most of the time.
2. The day I move into new housing I have chosen, I can be pretty sure that my new neighbors will be either neutral or pleasant to me.

3. I can go shopping alone most of the time, pretty well assured that I will not be followed or harassed by store detectives.

4. I can turn on the television or open to the front page of the paper and see people of my race widely and positively represented.

5. When I am told about our national heritage or about "civilization," I am shown that people of my color made it what it is.

6. I can be sure that my children will be given curricular materials that testify to the existence of their race, in every subject, at every grade level.

7. If I want to, I can be pretty sure of finding a publisher for this piece on white privilege.

8. I can go into a supermarket and find the staple foods which fit with my cultural traditions, into a hairdresser's shop and find someone who can cut my hair.

9. Whether I use a check, credit card, or cash, I can count on my skin color not to work against the appearance that I am financially reliable.

10. I could arrange to protect our children most of the time from people who might not like them.

11. I was able to teach our children that the town police were their allies and protectors.

12. I can swear, or dress in secondhand clothes, or not answer letters without having people attribute these choices to the bad morals, the poverty, or the illiteracy of my race.

13. I can speak in public to a powerful male group without putting my race on trial.

14. I can do well in a challenging situation without being called a credit to my race.

15. I am never asked to speak for all the people of my racial group.

16. I can remain oblivious of the language and customs of persons of color who constitute the world's majority without feeling in my culture any penalty for such oblivion.

17. I can criticize our government or talk about how much I fear its policies and behavior without being seen as a cultural outsider.

18. I can be pretty sure that if I ask to talk to "the person in charge," I will be facing a person of my race.

19. If a traffic cop pulls me over or if the IRS audits my tax return, I can be sure I haven't been singled out because of my race.

20. I can easily buy posters, postcards, picture books, greeting cards, dolls, toys, and children's magazines featuring people of my race.

21. I can go home from most meetings of organizations I belong to feeling somewhat tied in, rather than isolated, out-of-place, outnumbered, unheard, held at a distance, or feared.

22. I can take a job with an affirmative action employer without having coworkers on the job suspect that I got it because of race, or keep it because of my race.

23. I can choose public accommodation without fearing that people of my race cannot get in or will be mistreated in the places I have chosen.

24. I can be sure that if I need legal or medical help, my race will not work against me.

25. If my day, week, or year is going badly, I need not ask of each negative episode or situation whether it has racial overtones.

26. I can choose blemish cover or bandages in "flesh" color and have them more or less match my skin.

I repeatedly forgot each of the realizations on this list until I wrote it down. For me, white privilege has turned out to be an elusive and fugitive subject. The pressure to avoid it is great, for in facing it I must give up the myth of meritocracy. If these things are true, this is not such a free country; one's life is not what one makes it; many doors open for certain people through no virtues of their own.

In unpacking this invisible knapsack of white privilege, I have listed conditions of daily experience which I once took for granted. Nor did

I think of any of these perquisites as bad for the holder. I now think that we need a more finely differentiated taxonomy of privilege, for some of these varieties are only what one would want for everyone in a just society, and others give license to be ignorant, oblivious, arrogant, and destructive.

I see a pattern running through the matrix of white privilege, a pattern of assumptions which were passed on to me as a white person. There was one main piece of cultural turf; it was my own turf, and I was among those who could control the turf. *My skin color was an asset for any move I was educated to want to make*. I could think of myself as belonging in major ways, and of making social systems work for me. I could freely disparage, fear, neglect, or be oblivious to anything outside of the dominant cultural forms. Being of the main culture, I could also criticize it fairly freely.

In proportion, as my racial group was being made confident, comfortable, and oblivious, other groups were likely being made unconfident, uncomfortable, and alienated. Whiteness protected me from many kinds of hostility, distress, and violence, which I was being subtly trained to visit in turn upon people of color.

For this reason, the word "privilege" now seems to me misleading. We usually think of privilege as being a favored state, whether earned or conferred by birth or luck. Yet some of the conditions I have described here work to systematically overempower certain groups. Such privilege simply *confers dominance* because of one's race or sex.

I want, then, to distinguish between earned strength which is earned and unearned power which is conferred systemically. Power from unearned privilege can look like strength when it is in fact permission to escape or to dominate. But not all of the privileges on my list are inevitably damaging. Some, like the expectation that neighbors will be decent to you, or that your race will not count against you in court, should be the norm in a just society. Others, like the permission to ignore the least powerful people, distort the humanity of the holders as well as the ignored groups.

We might at least start by distinguishing between positive advantages which we can work to spread, and negative types of advantages which, unless rejected, will always reinforce our present hierarchies. For example, the feeling that one belongs within the human circle, as Native Americans say, should not be seen as privilege for a few. Ideally it is an *unearned entitlement*. At present, since only a few have it, it is an *unearned advantage* for them. This paper results from a process of coming to see that some of the power which I originally saw as attendant on being a human being in the United States consisted in *unearned advantage* and *conferred dominance*.

I have met very few men who are truly distressed about systemic, unearned male advantage and conferred dominance. And so one question for me and others like me is whether we will be like them, or whether we will get truly distressed, even outraged, about unearned race advantage and conferred dominance and, if so, what we will do to lessen them. In any case, we need to do more work in identifying how they actually affect our daily lives. Many, perhaps most, of our white students in the United States think that racism doesn't affect them because they are not people of color; they do not see "whiteness" as a racial identity. In addition, since race and sex are not the only advantaging systems at work, we need similarly to examine the daily experience of having age advantage, or ethnic advantage, or physical ability, or advantage related to nationality, class, religion, or sexual orientation.

Difficulties and dangers surrounding the task of finding parallels are many. Since racism, sexism, and heterosexism are not the same, the advantaging associated with them should not be seen as the same. In addition, it is hard to disentangle aspects of unearned advantage which rest more on social class, economic class, race, religion, sex, and ethnic identity than on other factors. Still, all of the oppressions are interlocking, as the Combahee River Collective Statement of 1977 continues to remind us eloquently.

One factor seems clear about all of the interlocking oppressions. They take both active forms which we can see and embedded forms which as a member of the dominant group one is taught not to see. In my class and place, I did not recognize myself as a racist because I was taught to see racism only in individual acts of meanness by members of my group, never in invisible systems conferring unsought racial dominance on my group from birth.

Disapproving of the systems won't be enough to change them. I was taught to think that racism could end if white individuals changed their attitudes. [But] a "white" skin in the United States opens many doors for whites whether or not we approve of the way dominance has been conferred on us. Individual acts can palliate, but cannot end, these problems.

To make systems equitable we need first to acknowledge their colossal unseen dimensions. The silences and denials surrounding privilege are the key political tool here. They keep the thinking about equality or equity incomplete, protecting unearned advantage and conferred dominance by making these taboo subjects. Most talk by whites about equal opportunity seems to me now to be about equal opportunity to try to get into a position of dominance while denying that *systems* of dominance exist.

It seems to me that obliviousness about white advantage, like obliviousness about male advantage, is kept strongly inculturated in the United States so as to maintain the myth of meritocracy, the myth that democratic choice is equally available to all. Keeping most people unaware that freedom of confident action is there for just a small number of people props up those in power and serves to keep power in the hands of the same groups that have most of it already.

Though systemic change takes many decades, there are pressing questions for me and I imagine for some others like me if we raise our daily consciousness on the perquisites of being light-skinned. What will we do with such knowledge? As we know from watching men, it is an open question whether we will choose to use unearned advantage to weaken hidden systems of advantage, or whether we will use any of our arbitrarily awarded power to try to reconstruct power systems on a broader base. It is not a matter for blame or guilt. We did not ask to be born into these systems. But having seen them, we can if we wish take some responsibility for using unearned power to share power.

bharati mukherjee

bharati mukherjee

Bharati Mukherjee was born in 1940 in Calcutta. She attended the universities of Calcutta and Baroda, where she received a master's degree in English and ancient Indian culture. In 1961, she came to the United States to attend the writer's workshop at the University of Iowa. She became an American citizen in 1988. Mukherjee is one of America's most daring writers of fiction. Her books include *The Tiger's Daughter, Middlemen and Other Stories*, which won the National Book Critics Award in 1989, *Jasmine*, and *The Holder of the World*. She has also written two books of nonfiction with her husband, Clark Blaise, *Days and Nights in Calcutta*, and *The Sorrow and the Terror*.

Currently a professor of English at the University of California, Berkeley, she lives in San Francisco.

beyond multiculturalism:
surviving the nineties

In these times of serious, often violent, cultural and ethnic identity crises that are tearing apart many nations, I am particularly thankful to have this opportunity to share with you—who are mostly second-, third-, fourth-generation descendants of European immigrants—my experiences as a non-European pioneer and my hopes for the future of the country you and I have chosen to live in.

The United States exists as a sovereign nation with its officially stated constitution, its economic and foreign policies, its demarcated, patrolled boundaries. "America," however, exists as image or idea, as dream or nightmare, as romance or plague, constructed by discrete individual fantasies, and shaded by collective paranoias and mythologies.

I am a naturalized U.S. citizen with a certificate of citizenship; more important, I am an American for whom "America" is the stage for the drama of self-transformation. I see American culture as a culture of dreamers, who believe material shape (which is not the same as materialism) can be given to dreams. They believe that one's station in life—poverty, education, family background—does not determine one's fate. They believe in the reversal of omens; early failures do not spell inevitable disaster. Outsiders can triumph on merit. All of this happens against the backdrop of the familiar vicissitudes of American life.

I first came to the United States—to the state of Iowa, to be precise—on a late summer evening nearly thirty-three years ago. I flew into a placid, verdant airport in Iowa City on a commercial airliner, ready to fulfill the goals written out in a large, lined notebook for me by my guiltlessly patriarchal father. Those goals were unambiguous: I was to spend two years studying Creative Writing at Paul Eagle's unique Writers' Workshop; then I was to marry the perfect Bengali bridegroom selected by [my father] and live out the rest of a contented, predictable life in the city of my birth, Calcutta. In 1961, I was a shy, pliant, well-mannered, dutiful young daughter from a very privileged, traditional mainstream Hindu family that believed that women should be protected and provided for by their fathers, husbands, sons, and it did not once occur to me that I might have goals of my own, quite distinct from those specified for me by my father. I certainly did not anticipate then that, over the next three decades, Iowans—who seemed to me so racially and culturally homogeneous—would be forced to shudder through the violent paroxysms of a collective identity in crisis.

When I was growing up in Calcutta in the fifties, I heard no talk of "identity crisis"—communal or individual. The concept itself—of a person not knowing who she or he was—was unimaginable in a hierarchical, classification-obsessed society. One's identity was absolutely fixed, derived from religion, caste, patrimony, and mother-tongue. A Hindu Indian's last name was designed to announce his or her forefathers' caste and place of origin. A Mukherjee could *only* be a Brahmin from Bengal. Indian tradition forbade intercaste, interlanguage, interethnic marriages. Bengali tradition discouraged even emigration; to remove oneself from Bengal was to "pollute" true culture.

Until the age of eight I lived in a house crowded with forty or fifty relatives. We lived together because we were "family," bonded by kinship, though kinship interpreted in flexible enough terms to include, when necessary, men, women, children who came from the same *desh*—which is the Bengali word for "homeland"—as had my father and grandfather. I was who I was because I was Dr. Sudhir Lal Mukherjee's daughter, because I was a Hindu Brahmin, because I was Bengali-speaking, and because my *desh* was an East Bengal village called Faridpur. I was encouraged to think of myself as indistinguishable from my dozen girl-cousins. Identity was viscerally connected with ancestral soil and family origins. I was first a Mukherjee, then a Bengali Brahmin, and only then an Indian.

Deep down I knew, of course, that I was not quite like my girl-cousins. Deeper down, I was sure that pride in the purity of one's culture has a sinister underside. As a child, I had witnessed bloody religious riots between Muslims and Hindus, and violent language riots between Bengalis and Biharis. People kill for culture, and die of hunger. Language, race, religion, blood, myth, history, national codes, and manners have all been used, in India, in the United States, are being used in Bosnia and Rwanda even today, to enforce terror, to otherize, to murder.

I do not know what compelled my strong-willed and overprotective father to risk sending us, his three daughters, to school in the United States, a country he had not visited. In Calcutta he had insisted on sheltering us from danger and temptation by sending us to girls-only schools, and by providing us chaperones, chauffeurs, and bodyguards.

The Writers' Workshop in a quonset hut in Iowa City was my first experience of coeducation. And after not too long, I fell in love with a fellow student named Clark Blaise, an American of Canadian origin, and impulsively married him during a lunch break in a lawyer's office above a coffee shop.

That impulsive act cut me off forever from the rules and ways of upper-middle-class life in Bengal, and hurled me precipitously into a New World life of scary improvisations and heady explorations. Until my lunchtime wedding, I had seen myself as an Indian foreign student, a transient in the United States. The five-minute ceremony in the lawyer's office had changed me into a permanent transient.

Over the last three decades the important lesson that I have learned is that in this era of massive diasporic movements, honorable survival requires resilience, curiosity, and compassion, a letting go of rigid ideals about the purity of inherited culture.

The first ten years into marriage, years spent mostly in my husband's *desh* of Canada, I thought myself an expatriate Bengali permanently stranded in North America because of a power surge of destiny or of desire. My first novel, *The Tiger's Daughter*, embodies the loneliness I felt but could not acknowledge, even to myself, as I negotiated the no-man's-land between the country of my past and the continent of my present. Shaped by memory, textured with nostalgia for a class and culture I had abandoned, this novel quite naturally became my expression of the *expatriate consciousness*.

It took me a decade of painful introspection to put the smothering tyranny of nostalgia in perspective, and to make the transition from expatriate to immigrant. I have found my way back to the United States after a fourteen-year stay in Canada. The transition from foreign student to U.S. citizen, from detached onlooker to committed immigrant, has not been easy.

The years in Canada were particularly harsh. Canada is a country that officially, and proudly, resists the policy and process of cultural fusion. For all its smug rhetoric about "cultural mosaic," Canada refuses to renovate its national self-image to include its changing complexion. It is a New World country with Old World concepts of a fixed, exclusivist national identity. And all through the seventies, when I lived there, it was a country without a Bill of Rights or its own Constitution. Canadian official rhetoric designated me, as a citizen of non-European origin, one of the "visible minority" who, even though I spoke the Canadian national languages of English and French, was straining "the absorptive capacity" of Canada. Canadians of color were routinely treated as "not real" Canadians. In fact, when a terrorist bomb, planted in an Air India jet on Canadian soil, blew up after leaving Montreal, killing 329 passengers, 90 percent of whom were Canadians of Indian origin, the then prime minister of Canada, Brian Mulroney, cabled the Indian prime minister to offer Canada's condolences for India's loss, exposing the Eurocentricity of the "mosaic" policy of immigration.

In private conversations, some Canadian ambassadors and External Affairs officials have admitted to me that the creation of the Ministry of Multiculturalism in the seventies was less an instrument for cultural tolerance and more a vote-getting strategy to pacify ethnic European constituents who were alienated by the rise of Quebec separatism and the simultaneous increase of nonwhite immigrants.

The years of race-related harassments in a Canada without a Constitution have politicized me, and deepened my love of the ideals embedded in the American Bill of Rights.

I take my American citizenship very seriously. I am a voluntary immigrant. I am not an economic refugee, and not a seeker of political asylum. I am an American by choice, and not by the simple accident of birth. I have made emotional, social, and political commitments to this country. I have earned the right to think of myself as an American.

But in this blood-splattered decade, questions such as who is an American and what is American culture are being posed with belligerence and being answered with violence. We are witnessing an increase in physical, too often fatal, assaults on Asian-Americans. An increase in systematic "dot-busting" of Indo-Americans in New Jersey, xenophobic immigrant-baiting in California, minority-on-minority violence during the south-central L.A. revolution.

America's complexion is browning daily. Journalists' surveys have established that whites are losing their clear majority status in some states, and have already lost it in New York and California. A recent *Time* magazine poll indicated that 60 percent of Americans favor limiting *legal* immigration. Eighty percent of Americans polled favor curbing the entry of undocumented aliens. U.S. borders are too extensive and too porous to be adequately policed. Immigration, by documented and undocumented aliens, is less affected by the U.S. Immigration and Naturalization Service, and more by wars, ethnic genocides, famines in the emigrant's own country.

Every sovereign nation has a right to formulate its immigration policy. In this decade of continual, large-scale diasporic movements, it is imperative that we come to some agreement about who "we" are now that the community includes old-timers, newcomers, many races

[and] languages and religions; about what our expectations of happiness and strategies for its pursuit are; and what our goals are for the nation.

Scapegoating of immigrants has been the politicians' easy instant remedy. Hate speeches fill auditoria, bring in megabucks for those demagogues willing to profit from stirring up racial animosity.

The hysteria against newcomers is only minimally generated by the downturn in our economy. The panic, I suspect, is unleashed by a fear of the Other, the fear of what Daniel Stein, the executive director of the Federation for American Immigration Reform and a champion of closed borders, is quoted as having termed "cultural transmogrification."

The debate about American culture has, to date, been monopolized by rabid Eurocentrists and ethnocentrists; the rhetoric has been flamboyantly divisive, pitting a phantom "us" against a demonized "them." I am here to launch a new discourse, to reconstitute the hostile biology-derived "us" versus "them" communities into a new *consensual* community of "we."

All countries view themselves by their ideals. Indians idealize, as well they should, the cultural continuum, the inherent value-system of India, and are properly incensed when foreigners see nothing but poverty, intolerance, ignorance, strife, and injustice. Americans see themselves as the embodiments of liberty, openness, and individualism, even when the world judges them for drugs, crime, violence, bigotry, militarism, and homelessness. I was in Singapore last month when the media were very vocal about the case of the American teenager sentenced to caning for having allegedly vandalized cars. The overwhelming local sentiment was that caning Michael Fay would deter local youths from being tempted into "Americanization," meaning into gleefully breaking laws.

Conversely, in Tavares, Florida, an ardently patriotic school board has legislated that middle school teachers be required to instruct their students that American culture, meaning European-American culture, is inherently "superior to other foreign or historic cultures." The sinister, or at least misguided, implication is that American culture has not been affected by the American Indian, African-American, Latin-American, and Asian-American segments of its population.

The idea of "America" as a nation has been set up in opposition to the tenet that a nation is a collection of like-looking, like-speaking, like-worshipping people. Our nation is unique in human history. We have seen in very recent weeks, in a Germany plagued with antiforeigner frenzy, how violently destabilizing the traditional concept of nation can be. In Europe, each country is, in a sense, a tribal homeland. Therefore, the primary criterion for nationhood in Europe is homogeneity of culture, and race, and religion. And that has contributed to blood-soaked balkanization in the former Yugoslavia and the former Soviet Union.

All European-Americans in this room, or their pioneering ancestors, gave up an easy homogeneity in their original countries for a new idea of utopia. What we have going for us in the 1990s is the exciting chance to share in the making of a new American culture rather than the coerced acceptance of either the failed nineteenth-century model of "melting pot" or the Canadian model of "the multicultural mosaic."

The "mosaic" implies a contiguity of self-sufficient, utterly distinct cultures. "Multiculturalism" has come to imply the existence of a central culture, ringed by peripheral cultures. The sinister fallout of official multiculturalism and of professional multiculturists is the establishment of one culture as the norm and the rest as aberrations. Multiculturalism emphasizes the differences between racial heritages. This emphasis on the differences has too often led to the dehumanization of the different. And dehumanization leads to discrimination. And discrimination can ultimately lead to genocide.

We need to alert ourselves to the limitations and the dangers of those discourses that reinforce an "us" versus "them" mentality. We need to protest any official rhetoric or demagoguery that marginalizes on a race-related and/or religion-related basis any segment of our society. I want to discourage the retention of cultural memory if the aim of that retention is cultural balkanization. I want to sensitize you to think of culture and nationhood *not* as an uneasy aggregate of antagonistic *thems* and *uses*, but as a constantly re-forming, transmogrifying "we."

In this diasporic age, one's biological identity may not be the only one. Erosions and accretions come with the act of emigration.

The experiences of violent unhousement from a biological "homeland" and rehousement in an adopted "homeland" that is not always welcoming to its dark-complexioned citizens have tested me as a person, and made me the writer I am today.

I choose to describe myself on my own terms, that is, as an American without hyphens. It is to sabotage the politics of hate and the campaigns of revenge spawned by Eurocentric patriots on the one hand and the professional multiculturalists on the other that I describe myself as an American rather than as an Asian-American. Why is it that hyphenization is imposed only on nonwhite Americans? And why is it that only nonwhite citizens are "problematized" if they choose to describe themselves on their own terms? My outspoken rejection of hyphenization is my lonely campaign to obliterate categorizing the cultural landscape into a "center" and its "peripheries." To reject hyphenization is to demand that the nation deliver the promises of the American Dream and the American Constitution to *all* its citizens. I want nothing less than to invent a new vocabulary that demands, and obtains, an equitable power-sharing for all members of the American community.

But my self-empowering refusal to be "otherized" and "objectified" has come at tremendous cost. My rejection of hyphenization has been deliberately misrepresented as "race treachery" by some India-born, urban, upper-middle-class Marxist green-card holders with lucrative Chairs on U.S. campuses. These academics strategically position themselves as self-appointed spokespersons for their ethnic communities, and as guardians of the "purity" of ethnic cultures. At the same time, though they reside permanently in the United States and participate in the capitalist economy of this nation, they publicly denounce

American ideals and institutions. They direct their rage at me because, as a U.S. citizen, I have invested in the present and the future rather than in the expatriate's imagined homeland. They condemn me because I acknowledge erosion of memory as a natural result of emigration, because I count that erosion as net gain rather than as loss, and because I celebrate racial and cultural "mongrelization." I have no respect for these expatriate fence-straddlers who, even while competing fiercely for tenure and promotion within the U.S. academic system, glibly equate all evil in the world with the United States, capitalism, colonialism, and corporate and military expansionism. I regard the artificial retentions of "pure race" and "pure culture" as dangerous, reactionary illusions fostered by the Eurocentric and the ethnocentric empire-builders within the academy. I fear still more the politics of revenge preached from pulpits by some minority demagogues.

People who choose to reside permanently in the United States but who refuse to share the responsibility entailed in taking out American citizenship should not presume to speak for, let alone condemn, those of us who have accepted the psychological, social, political transformations and responsibilities necessitated by naturalization.

As a writer, my literary agenda begins by acknowledging that America has transformed *me*. It does not end until I show that I (and the hundreds of thousands of recent immigrants like me) are minute-by-minute transforming America. The transformation is a two-way process; it affects both the individual and the national-cultural identity. The end result of immigration, then, is this two-way transformation: that's my heartfelt message.

Others often talk of diaspora, of arrival as the end of the process. They talk of arrival in the context of loss, the loss of communal memory and the erosion of an intact ethnic culture. They use words like "erosion" and "loss" in alarmist ways. I want to talk of arrival as gain. Both Salman Rushdie and I see immigration as a process of self-integration.

What excites me is that we have the chance to retain those values we treasure from our original cultures, but that we also acknowledge that the outer forms of those values are likely to change. In the Indian-American community, I see a great deal of guilt about the inability to hang on to "pure culture." Parents express rage or despair at their U.S.-born children's forgetting of, or indifference to, some aspects of Indian culture. Of those parents I would ask: What is it we have lost if our children are acculturating into the culture in which we are living? Is it so terrible that our children are discovering or inventing homelands for themselves? Some first-generation Indo-Americans, embittered by overt anti-Asian racism and by unofficial "glass ceilings," construct a phantom more-Indian-than-Indians-in-India identity as defense against marginalization. Of them I would ask: Why not get actively involved in fighting discrimination through protests and lawsuits?

I prefer that we forge a national identity that is born of our acknowledgment of the steady de-Europeanization of the U.S. population, and which constantly synthesizes—*fuses*—the disparate cultures of our country's residents, and that provides a new, sustaining, and unifying national creed.

reverend cecil b. williams

reverend cecil b. williams

Reverend Cecil B. Williams was born in 1929 and grew up in the segregated town of San Angelo, Texas. In his family he was nicknamed Rev, a shortened reference to the ministry that was, according to Williams, "the highest praise and heaviest pressure that a churchgoing family could place on one of its sons." It seemed preordained that he would become a bishop one day in the black Methodist conference. But during the summer when he turned ten, Williams had a nervous breakdown, occasioned by the virulence of the racism in the town that surrounded him. When he recovered, he swore that he would never live by the rules of segregation.

Reverend Williams moved to San Francisco in 1963, as the director of community involvement for the Glide Foundation. He became minister of Glide Church in 1966 and in the next thirty years has transformed it from a small and dwindling congregation in the city's tough Tenderloin neighborhood into one of the most vital churches in America, serving the needs of neighborhood residents and attracting people throughout the Bay Area to the Sunday "Celebrations." Glide has become the most comprehensive nonprofit provider of human services in San Francisco.

Reverend Williams is the author, with Rebecca Laird, of *No Hiding Place: Empowerment and Recovery for our Troubled Communities.*

a sermon at glide

Yes, this is a freaky place. There is no fantasyland when you come [to Glide], there are no illusions when you come in here, there is no put-on when you come in here. What you see is what you get. What you talk is what you get. What you walk is what you get. What you sing is what you get. What you embrace is what you get. This is humanity. All of humanity, getting together, saying, Here we are, being real for a change, with everybody. We are originals. We go back to that which is our roots, and we dig deep into our roots and till the soil of the roots so that we can grow and change, and stop denying and stop lying and putting-on, and stop acting like we're something we're not. We are here.

We are not a fancy group of different races and cultures and ages coming together; this is not fancy. This is real, y'all. We're freaks because we choose not to go by the rules. The church says that we gotta be always nice and sweet and kind and lying and denying. We get mad here, we get angry here. They say that Jesus was a madman.

We have a common hope that empowers people everywhere. Sometimes people will ask me: Where'd you get all that hope? I know that the darker it is, the more awful it is, that the greater the hardship, that when you're ready to go to the Golden Gate Bridge; or you're suffering from an incurable disease; or you're being floated across the southern tip of Florida trying to make it to some kind of land, to some kind of source, and you have no home, no place to go back to; or you live in the "hood" in urban America, or suburbia, or wherever you live; I know this—that the human condition can always have hope where two or three are gathered together. Because where we come together, it is there that we find not only our great differences but our great common pain and hurt, love and concern, our great humanity. It is out of that that hope comes. Because God has said, stop trying to catch me, I'm after you.

You don't even know who you're sitting by this morning. There could be somebody sitting beside you who's been in prison for thirty years, and just got out yesterday. There could be somebody from Pacific Heights who has a four- or five-million-dollar home, sitting here, who just got out of prison, but don't worry who's beside you, not in this church. We were thrilled that Jerry Brown came here, that Bill Clinton came here, lot of other famous folks have come here. Somebody asked me: Well, would you let President Bush come to Glide? I said, Hey, President Bush needs Glide.

Henry Thoreau has said that what we must find out is not what was but what is. And then he says that where a battle has been fought, you will find nothing but the bones of men and beasts, but where a battle is being fought, there are hearts still beating. And here at Glide today there are hearts still beating. This is the battleground, out there is the battleground. Wherever there is humanity, wherever people are being oppressed, wherever starvation is occurring, wherever people are jobless, or homeless, wherever people have no understanding of themselves and what they must do, not only in the "hood" and the ghettos, and the barrios, not only in the concentration camps, but also in suburbia, there are people who are in great need. They may have material things, but when it comes to hope, they don't have much hope. And here we are gathered to let them know that we bring hope to the world, and we bring hope to ourselves.

henry louis gates, jr.

thirteen ways of looking
at a black man

*A different kind of jury—one made up of black cultural leaders—weighs in
on the Simpson verdict and the Million Man March.*

"Every day, in every way, we are getting meta and meta," the
philosopher John Wisdom used to say, venturing a cultural counter-
part to Emile Coué's famous mantra of self-improvement. So it makes
sense that in the aftermath of the Simpson trial the focus of attention
has been swiftly displaced from the verdict to the reaction to the verdict, and then to the reaction to the reaction to the verdict, and, finally, to the reaction to the reaction to the reaction to the
verdict—which is to say, black indignation at white anger at black ju-
bilation at Simpson's acquittal. It's a spiral made possible by the relay
circuit of race. Only in America.

An American historian I know registers a widespread sense of
bathos when he says, "Who would have imagined that the Simpson
trial would be like the Kennedy assassination—that you'd remember
where you were when the verdict was announced?" But everyone
does, of course. The eminent sociologist William Julius Wilson was in
the red-carpet lounge of a United Airlines terminal, the only black in
a crowd of white travelers, and found himself as stunned and dis-

turbed as they were. Wynton Marsalis, on tour with his band in California, recalls that "everybody was acting like they were above watching it, but then when it got to be ten o'clock—zoom, we said, 'Put the verdict on!' " Spike Lee was with Jackie Robinson's widow, Rachel, rummaging through a trunk filled with her husband's belongings, in preparation for a bio-pic he's making on the athlete. Jamaica Kincaid was sitting in her car in the parking lot of her local grocery store in Vermont, listening to the proceedings on National Public Radio, and she didn't pull out until after they were over. I was teaching a literature seminar at Harvard from twelve to two, and watched the verdict with the class on a television set in the seminar room. That's where I first saw the sort of racialized response that itself would fill television screens for the next few days: the white students looked aghast, and the black students cheered. "Maybe you should remind the students that this is a case about two people who were brutally slain, and not an occasion to celebrate," my teaching assistant, a white woman, whispered to me.

The two weeks spanning the O. J. Simpson verdict and Louis Farrakhan's Million Man March on Washington were a good time for connoisseurs of racial paranoia. As blacks exulted at Simpson's acquittal, horrified whites had a fleeting sense that this race thing was knottier than they'd ever supposed—that, when all the pieties were cleared away, blacks really *were* strangers in their midst. (The unspoken sentiment: *And I thought I knew these people.*) There was the faintest tincture of the southern slave-owner's disquiet in the aftermath of the bloody slave revolt led by Nat Turner—when the gentleman farmer was left to wonder which of his smiling, servile retainers would have slit *his* throat if the rebellion had spread as was intended, like fire on parched thatch. In the day or so following the verdict, young urban professionals took note of a slight *froideur* between themselves and their nannies and baby-sitters—the awkwardness of an unbroached subject. Rita Dove, who recently completed a term as the U.S. Poet Laureate, and who believes that Simpson was guilty, found it "appalling that white people were so outraged—more appalling than the decision as to whether he was guilty or not." Of course, it's possible to overstate the tensions. Marsalis invokes the example of team sports, saying, "You want your side to win, whatever the side is going to be. And the thing is, we're still at a point in our national history where we look at each other as sides."

The matter of side-taking cuts deep. An old cartoon depicts a woman who has taken her errant daughter to see a child psychiatrist. "And when we were watching *The Wizard of Oz*," the distraught mother is explaining, "she was rooting for the wicked witch!" What many whites experienced was the bewildering sense that an entire population had been rooting for the wrong side. "This case is a classic example of what I call interstitial spaces," says Judge A. Leon Higginbotham, who recently retired from the federal Court of Appeals, and who last month received the Presidential Medal of Freedom. "The jury system is predicated on the idea that different people can view the same evidence and reach diametrically opposed conclusions." But the observation brings little solace. If we disagree about something so basic, how can we find agreement about far thornier matters? For white observers, what's even scarier than the idea that black Americans were plumping for the villain, which is a misprision of value, is the idea that black Americans didn't recognize him *as* the villain, which is a misprision of fact. How can conversation begin when we disagree about reality? To put it at its harshest, for many whites a sincere belief in Simpson's innocence looks less like the culture of protest than like the culture of psychosis.

Perhaps you didn't know that Liz Claiborne appeared on *Oprah* not long ago and said that she didn't design her clothes for black women—that their hips were too wide. Perhaps you didn't know that the soft drink Tropical Fantasy is manufactured by the Ku Klux Klan and contains a special ingredient designed to sterilize black men. (A warning flyer distributed in Harlem a few years ago claimed that these findings were vouchsafed on the television program *20/20*.) Perhaps you didn't know that the Ku Klux Klan has a similar arrangement with Church's Fried Chicken—or is it Popeye's?

Perhaps you didn't know these things, but a good many black Americans think they do, and will discuss them with the same intentness they bring to speculations about the "shadowy figure" in a Brentwood driveway. Never mind that Liz Claiborne has never appeared on *Oprah*, that the beleaguered Brooklyn company that makes Tropical Fantasy has gone as far as to make available an FDA assay of its ingredients, and that those fried-chicken franchises pose a threat mainly to black folks' arteries. The folklorist Patricia A. Turner, who has collected dozens of such tales in an invaluable 1993 study of rumor in African-American culture, "I Heard It Through the Grapevine," points out the patterns to be found here: that these stories encode regnant anxieties, that they take root under particular conditions and play particular social roles, that the currency of rumor flourishes where "official" news has proved untrustworthy.

Certainly the Fuhrman tapes might have been scripted to confirm the old saw that paranoids, too, have enemies. If you wonder why blacks seem particularly susceptible to rumors and conspiracy theories, you might look at a history in which the official story was a poor guide to anything that mattered much, and in which rumor sometimes verged on the truth. Heard the one about the L.A. cop who hated interracial couples, fantasized about making a bonfire of black bodies, and boasted of planting evidence? How about the one about the federal government's forty-year study of how untreated syphilis affects black men? For that matter, have you ever read through some of the FBI's cointelpro files? ("There is but one way out for you," an FBI scribe wrote to Martin Luther King, Jr., in 1964, thoughtfully urging on him the advantages of suicide. "You better take it before your filthy, abnormal, fraudulent self is bared to the nation.")

People arrive at an understanding of themselves and the world through narratives—narratives purveyed by schoolteachers, newscasters, "authorities," and all the other authors of our common sense.

Counternarratives are, in turn, the means by which groups contest that dominant reality and the fretwork of assumptions that supports it. Sometimes delusion lies that way, sometimes not. There's a sense in which much of black history is simply counternarrative that has been documented and legitimatized, by slow, hard-won scholarship. The "shadowy figures" of American history have long been our own ancestors, both free and enslaved. In any case, fealty to counternarratives is an index to alienation, not to skin color: witness Representative Helen Chenoweth of Idaho and her devoted constituents. With all the oppositeness of allegory, the copies of *The Protocols of the Elders of Zion* sold by black vendors in New York—who are supplied with them by Lushena Books, a black-nationalist book wholesaler—were published by the white supremacist Angriff Press, in Hollywood. Paranoia knows no color or coast.

Finally, though, it's misleading to view counternarrative as another pathology of disenfranchisement. If the MIA myth, say, is rooted among a largely working-class constituency, there are many myths— one of them known as Reaganism—that hold considerable appeal among the privileged classes. "So many white brothers and sisters are living in a state of denial in terms of how deep white supremacy is seated in their culture and society," the scholar and social critic Cornel West says. "Now we recognize that in a fundamental sense we really do live in different worlds." In that respect, the reaction to the Simpson verdict has been something of an education. The novelist Ishmael Reed talks of "wealthy white male commentators who live in a world where the police don't lie, don't plant evidence—and drug dealers give you unlimited credit." He adds, "Nicole, you know, also dated Mafia hit men."

"I think he's innocent, I really do," West says. "I do think it was linked to some drug subculture of violence. It looks as if both O.J. and Nicole had some connection to drug activity. And the killings themselves were classic examples of that drug culture of violence. It could have to do with money owed—it could have to do with a number of things. And I think that O.J. was quite aware of and fearful of this." On this theory, Simpson may have appeared at the crime scene as a witness. "I think that he had a sense that it was coming down, both on him and on her, and Brother Ron Goldman just happened to be there," West conjectures. "But there's a possibility also that O.J. could have been there, gone over and tried to see what was going on, saw that he couldn't help, split, and just ran away. He might have said, 'I can't stop this thing, and they are coming at me to do the same thing.' He may have actually run for his life."

To believe that Simpson is innocent is to believe that a terrible injustice has been averted, and this is precisely what many black Americans, including many prominent ones, do believe. Thus the soprano Jessye Norman is angry over what she sees as the decision of the media to prejudge Simpson rather than "educate the public as to how we could possibly look at things a bit differently." She says she wishes that the real culprit "would stand up and say, 'I did this and I am sorry I caused so much trouble.' " And while she is sensitive to the issue of spousal abuse, she is skeptical about the way it was enlisted by the prosecution: "You have to stop getting into how they were at home, because there are not a lot of relationships that could be put on television that we would think, OK, that's a good one. I mean, just stop pretending that this is the case." Then, too, she asks, "Isn't it interesting to you that this Faye Resnick person was staying with Nicole Brown Simpson and that she happened to have left on the eighth of June? Does that tell you that maybe there's some awful coincidence here?" The widespread theory about murderous drug dealers Norman finds "perfectly plausible, knowing what drugs do," and she adds, "People are punished for being bad."

There's a sense in which all such accounts can be considered counternarratives, or fragments of them—subaltern knowledge, if you like. They dispute the tenets of official culture; they do not receive the imprimatur of editorialists or of network broadcasters; they are not seriously entertained on *MacNeil/Lehrer*. And when they do surface they are given consideration primarily for their ethnographic value. An official culture treats their claims as it does those of millenarian cultists in Texas, or Marxist deconstructionists in the academy: as things to be diagnosed, deciphered, given meaning—that is, *another* meaning. Black folk say they believe Simpson is innocent, and then the white gatekeepers of a media culture cajolingly explain what black folk really mean when they say it, offering the explanation from the highest of motives: because the alternative is a population that, by their lights, is not merely counternormative but crazy. Black folk may mean anything at all; just not what they say they mean.

Yet you need nothing so grand as an epistemic rupture to explain why different people weigh the evidence of authority differently. In the words of the cunning Republican campaign slogan, "Who do you trust?" It's a commonplace that white folks trust the police and black folks don't. Whites recognize this in the abstract, but they're continually surprised at the *depth* of black wariness. They shouldn't be. Norman Podhoretz's soul-searching 1963 essay, "My Negro Problem, and Ours"—one of the frankest accounts we have of liberalism and race resentment—tells of a Brooklyn boyhood spent under the shadow of carefree, cruel Negro assailants, and of the author's residual unease when he passes groups of blacks in his Upper West Side neighborhood. And yet, he notes in a crucial passage, "I know now, as I did not know when I was a child, that power is on my side, that the police are working for me and not for them." That ordinary, unremarkable comfort—the feeling that "the police are working for me"—continues to elude blacks, even many successful blacks. Thelma Golden, the curator of the Whitney Museum's "Black Male" show, points out that on the very day the verdict was announced a black man in Harlem was killed by the police under disputed circumstances. As older blacks like to repeat, "When white folks say 'justice,' they mean 'just us.' "

Blacks—in particular, black men—swap their experiences of police encounters like war stories, and there are few who don't have more than one story to tell. "These stories have a ring of cliché about them," Erroll McDonald, Pantheon's executive editor and one of the few prominent blacks in publishing, says, "but, as we all know about clichés, they're almost always true." McDonald tells of renting a Jaguar in New Orleans and being stopped by the police—simply "to show cause why I shouldn't be deemed a problematic Negro in a possibly stolen car." Wynton Marsalis says, "Shit, the police slapped me upside the head when I was in high school. I wasn't Wynton Marsalis then. I was just another nigger standing out somewhere on the street whose head could be slapped and did get slapped." The crime novelist Walter Mosley recalls, "When I was a kid in Los Angeles, they used to stop me all the time, beat on me, follow me around, tell me that I was stealing things." Nor does William Julius Wilson—who has a son-in-law on the Chicago police force ("You couldn't find a nicer, more dedicated guy")—wonder why he was stopped near a small New England town by a policeman who wanted to know what he was doing in those parts. There's a moving violation that many African-Americans know as DWB: Driving While Black.

So we all have our stories. In 1968, when I was eighteen, a man who knew me was elected mayor of my West Virginia county, in an upset victory. A few weeks into his term, he passed on something he thought I should know: The county police had made a list of people to be arrested in the event of a serious civil disturbance, and my name was on it. Years of conditioning will tell. Wynton Marsalis says, "My worst fear is to have to go before the criminal-justice system." Absurdly enough, it's mine, too.

Another barrier to interracial comprehension is talk of the "race card"—a phrase that itself infuriates many blacks. Judge Higginbotham, who pronounces himself "not uncomfortable at all" with the verdict, is uncomfortable indeed with charges that Johnnie Cochran played the race card. "This whole point is one hundred percent inaccurate," Higginbotham says. "If you knew that the most important witness had a history of racism and hostility against black people, that should have been a relevant factor of inquiry even if the jury had been all white. If the defendant had been Jewish and the police officer had a long history of expressed anti-Semitism and having planted evidence against innocent persons who were Jewish, I can't believe that anyone would have been saying that defense counsel was playing the anti-Semitism card." Angela Davis finds the very metaphor to be a problem. "Race is not a card," she says firmly. "The whole case was pervaded with issues of race."

Those who share her view were especially outraged at Robert Shapiro's famous post-trial rebuke to Cochran—for not only playing the race card but dealing it "from the bottom of the deck." Ishmael Reed, who is writing a book about the case, regards Shapiro's remarks as sheer opportunism: "He wants to keep his Beverly Hills clients—a perfectly commercial reason." In Judge Higginbotham's view, "Johnnie Cochran established that he was as effective as any lawyer in America, and though whites can tolerate black excellence in singing, dancing, and dunking, there's always been a certain level of discomfort among many whites when you have a one-on-one challenge in terms of intellectual competition. If Edward Bennett Williams, who was one of the most able lawyers in the country, had raised the same issues, half of the complaints would not exist."

By the same token, the display of black prowess in the courtroom was heartening for many black viewers. Cornel West says, "I think part of the problem is that Shapiro—and this is true of certain white brothers—has a profound fear of black-male charisma. And this is true not only in the law but across the professional world. You see, you have so many talented white brothers who deserve to be in the limelight. But one of the reasons they are not in the limelight is that they are not charismatic. And here comes a black person who's highly talented but also charismatic and therefore able to command center stage. So you get a very real visceral kind of jealousy that has to do with sexual competition as well as professional competition."

Erroll McDonald touches upon another aspect of sexual tension when he says, "The so-called race card has always been the joker. And the joker is the history of sexual racial politics in this country. People forget the singularity of this issue—people forget that less than a century ago black men were routinely lynched for merely glancing at white women or for having been *thought* to have glanced at a white woman." He adds, with mordant irony, "Now we've come to a point in our history where a black man could, potentially, have murdered a white woman and thrown in a white man to boot—and got off. So the country has become far more complex in its discussion of race." This is, as he appreciates, a less than perfectly consoling thought.

"But he's coming for me," a woman muses in Toni Morrison's 1994 novel *Jazz*, shortly before she is murdered by a jealous ex-lover. "Maybe tomorrow he'll find me. Maybe tonight." Morrison, it happens, is less interested in the grand passions of love and requital than she is in the curious texture of communal amnesty. In the event, the woman's death goes unavenged; the man who killed her is forgiven even by her friends and relatives. Neighbors feel that the man fell victim to her wiles, that he didn't understand "how she liked to push people, men." Or, as one of them says of her, "live the life; pay the price." Even the woman—who refuses to name the culprit as she bleeds to death—seems to accede to the view that she brought it on herself.

It's an odd and disturbing theme, and one with something of a history in black popular culture. An R & B hit from 1960, "There's Something on Your Mind," relates the anguish of a man who is driven to kill by his lover's infidelity. The chorus alternates with spoken narrative, which informs us that his first victim is the friend with whom she was unfaithful.

But then:

> Just as you make it up in your mind to forgive her, here come another one of your best friends through the door. This really makes you blow your top, and you go right ahead and shoot her. And realizing what you've done, you say: "Baby, please, speak to me. Forgive me. I'm sorry."

"We are a *forgiving* people," Anita Hill tells me, and she laughs, a little uneasily. We're talking about the support for O. J. Simpson in the black community; at least, I think we are.

A black woman told the *Times* last week, "He has been punished enough." But forgiveness is not all. There is also an element in this of outlaw culture: the tendency—which unites our lumpen proles with our postmodern ironists—to celebrate transgression for its own sake. Spike Lee, who was surprised but "wasn't happy" at the verdict ("I would have bet money that he was going to the slammer"), reached a similar conclusion: "A lot of black folks said, 'Man, O.J. is *bad*, you know. This is the first brother in the history of the world who got away with the murder of white folks, and a blond, blue-eyed woman at that.' "

But then there is the folk wisdom on the question of why Nicole Brown Simpson had to die—the theodicy of the streets. For nothing could be further from the outlaw ethic than the simple and widely shared certainty that, as Jessye Norman says, people are punished for doing wrong. And compounding the sentiment is Morrison's subject—the culturally vexed status of the so-called crime of passion, or what some took to be one, anyway. You play, you pay: It's an attitude that exists on the streets, but not only on the streets, and one that somehow attaches to Nicole, rather than to her ex-husband. Many counternarratives revolved around her putative misbehavior. The black feminist Bell Hooks notes with dismay that what many people took to be a "narrative of a crime of passion" had as its victim "a woman that many people, white and black, felt was like a whore. Precisely by being a sexually promiscuous woman, by being a woman who used drugs, by being a white woman with a black man, she had already fallen from grace in many people's eyes—there was no way to redeem her." Ishmael Reed, for one, has no interest in redeeming her. "To paint O. J. Simpson as a beast, they had to depict her as a saint," he complains. "Apparently, she had a violent temper. She slapped her Jamaican maid. I'm wondering, the feminists who are giving Simpson such a hard time—do they approve of white women slapping maids?"

• • •

Of course, the popular trial of Nicole Brown Simpson—one conducted off camera, in whispers—has further occluded anything recognizable as sexual politics. When Anita Hill heard that O. J. Simpson was going to be part of the Million Man March on Washington, she felt it was entirely in keeping with the occasion: A trial in which she believed matters of gender had been "bracketed" was going to be succeeded by a march from which women were excluded. And, while Minister Louis Farrakhan had told black men that October 16 was to serve as a "day of atonement" for their sins, the murder of Nicole Brown Simpson and Ronald Goldman was obviously not among the sins he had in mind. Bell Hooks argues, "Both O.J.'s case and the Million Man March confirm that, while white men are trying to be sensitive and pretending they're the new man, black men are saying that patriarchy must be upheld at all costs, even if women must die." She sees the march as a congenial arena for Simpson in symbolic terms: "I think he'd like to strut his stuff, as the patriarch. He is the dick that stayed hard longer." ("The surprising thing is that you won't see Clarence Thomas going on that march," Anita Hill remarks of another icon of patriarchy.) Farrakhan himself prefers metaphors of military mobilization, but the exclusionary politics of the event has clearly distracted from its ostensible message of solidarity. "First of all, I wouldn't go to no war and leave half the army home," says Amiri Baraka, the radical poet and playwright who achieved international renown in the sixties as the leading spokesman for the Black Arts movement. "Logistically, that doesn't make sense." He notes that Martin Luther King's 1963 March on Washington was "much more inclusive," and sees Farrakhan's regression as "an absolute duplication of what's happening in the country," from Robert Bly on: the sacralization of masculinity.

Something like that dynamic is what many white feminists saw on display in the Simpson verdict, but it's among women that the racial divide is especially salient. The black legal scholar and activist Patricia

Williams says she was "stunned by the intensely personal resentment of some of my white women friends in particular." Stunned but, on reflection, not mystified. "This is Greek drama," she declares. "Two of the most hotly contended aspects of our lives are violence among human beings who happen to be police officers and violence among human beings who happen to be husbands, spouses, lovers." Meanwhile, our attention has been fixated on the rhetorical violence between human beings who happen to disagree about the outcome of the O. J. Simpson trial.

It's a cliché to speak of the Simpson trial as a soap opera—as entertainment, as theater—but it's also true, and in ways that are worth exploring further. For one thing, the trial provides a fitting rejoinder to those who claim that we live in an utterly fragmented culture, bereft of the common narratives that bind a people together. True, Parson Weems has given way to Dan Rather, but public narrative persists. Nor has it escaped notice that the biggest televised legal contests of the last half decade have involved race matters: Anita Hill and Rodney King. So there you have it: the Simpson trial—black entertainment television at its finest. Ralph Ellison's hopeful insistence on the Negro's centrality to American culture finds, at last, a certain tawdry confirmation.

"The media generated in people a feeling of being spectators at a show," the novelist John Edgar Wideman says. "And at the end of a show you applaud. You are happy for the good guy. There is that sense of primal identification and closure." Yet it's a fallacy of "cultural literacy" to equate shared narratives with shared meanings. The fact that American TV shows are rebroadcast across the globe causes many people to wring their hands over the menace of cultural imperialism; seldom do they bother to inquire about the meanings that different people bring to and draw from these shows. When they do make inquiries, the results are often surprising. One researcher talked to Israeli Arabs who had just watched an episode of *Dallas*—an episode in which Sue Ellen takes her baby, leaves her husband, J.R., and moves in with her ex-lover and his father. The Arab viewers placed their own construction on the episode: They were all convinced that Sue Ellen had moved in with her *own* father—something that by their mores at least made sense.

A similar thing happened in America this year: The communal experience afforded by a public narrative (and what narrative more public?) was splintered by the politics of interpretation. As far as the writer Maya Angelou is concerned, the Simpson trial was an exercise in minstrelsy. "Minstrel shows caricatured every aspect of the black man's life, beginning with his sexuality," she says. "They portrayed the black man as devoid of all sensibilities and sensitivities. They minimized and diminished the possibility of familial love. And that is what the trial is about. Not just the prosecution but everybody seemed to want to show him as other than a normal human being. Nobody let us just see a man." But there is, of course, little consensus about what genre would best accommodate the material. Walter Mosley says, "The story plays to large themes, so I'm sure somebody will write about it. But I don't think it's a mystery. I think it's much more like a novel by Zola." What a writer might make of the material is one thing; what the audience has made of it is another.

"Simpson is a B-movie star and people were watching this like a B movie," Patricia Williams says. "And this is *not* the American B-movie ending." Or was it? "From my perspective as an attorney, this trial was much more like a movie than a trial," says Kathleen Cleaver, who was once the Black Panthers' minister for communication and is now a professor of law at Emory. "It had the budget of a movie, it had the casting of a movie, it had the tension of a movie, and the happy ending of a movie." Spike Lee, speaking professionally, is dubious about the trial's cinematic possibilities: "I don't care who makes this movie, it is never going to equal what people have seen in their living rooms and houses for eight or nine months." Or is it grand opera? Jessye Norman considers: "Well, it certainly has all the ingredients. I mean, somebody meets somebody and somebody gets angry with somebody and somebody dies." She laughs. "It sounds like the 'Ring' cycle of Wagner—it really does."

"This story has been told any number of times," Angelou says. "The first thing I thought about was Eugene O'Neill's *All God's Chillun*." Then she considers how the event might be retrieved by an African-American literary tradition. "I think a great writer would have to approach it," she tells me pensively. "James Baldwin could have done it. And Toni Morrison could do it."

"Maya Angelou could do it," I say

"I don't like that kind of stuff," she replies.

There are some for whom the question of adaptation is not entirely abstract. The performance artist and playwright Anna Deavere Smith has already worked on the 911 tape and F. Lee Bailey's cross-examination of Mark Fuhrman in the drama classes she teaches at Stanford. Now, with a dramaturge's eye, she identifies what she takes to be the climactic moment: "Just after the verdict was read I will always remember two sounds and one image. I heard Johnnie Cochran go 'Ugh,' and then I heard the weeping of Kim Goldman. And then I saw the image of O.J.'s son, with one hand going upward on one eye and one hand pointed down, shaking and sobbing. I couldn't do the words right now; if I could find a collaborator, I would do something else. I feel that a choreographer ought to do that thing. Part of the tragedy was the fact of that 'Ugh' and that crying. Because that 'Ugh' wasn't even a full sound of victory, really." In "Thirteen Ways of Looking at a Blackbird," Wallace Stevens famously said he didn't know whether he preferred "The beauty of inflections / Or the beauty of innuendoes, / The blackbird whistling / Or just after." American culture has spoken as with one voice: We like it just after.

Just after is when our choices and allegiances are made starkly apparent. Just after is when interpretation can be detached from the thing interpreted. Anita Hill, who saw her own presence at the Clarence Thomas hearings endlessly analyzed and allegorized, finds plenty of significance in the trial's reception, but says the trial itself had none. Naturally, the notion that the trial was sui generis is alien to most commentators. Yet it did not arrive in the world already costumed as a racial drama; it had to be racialized. And those critics—angry whites, indignant blacks—who like to couple this verdict with the Rodney King verdict should consider an elementary circumstance: Rodney King was an unknown and undistinguished black man who was brutalized by the police; the only thing exceptional about that episode was the presence of a video camera. But, as Bell Hooks asks, "in what other case have we ever had a wealthy black man being tried for murder?" Rodney King was a black man to his captors before he was anything else; O. J. Simpson was, first and foremost, O. J. Simpson. Kathleen Cleaver observes, "A black superhero millionaire is not someone for whom mistreatment is an issue." And Spike Lee acknowledges that the police "don't really bother black people once they are a personality." On this point, I'm reminded of something that Roland Gift, the lead singer of the pop group Fine Young Cannibals, once told a reporter: "I'm not black, I'm famous."

Simpson, too, was famous rather than black; that is, until the African-American community took its lead from the cover of *Time* and, well, blackened him. Some intellectuals are reluctant to go along with the conceit. Angela Davis, whose early-seventies career as a fugitive and a political prisoner provides one model of how to be famous *and* black, speaks of the need to question the way "O. J. Simpson serves as the generic black man," given that "he did not identify himself as black before then." More bluntly, Baraka says, "To see him get all of this God-damned support from people he has historically and steadfastly eschewed just pissed me off. He eschewed black people all his life and then, like Clarence Thomas, the minute he gets jammed up he comes talking about 'Hey, I'm black.' " And the matter of spousal abuse should remind us of another role-reversal entailed by Simpson's iconic status in a culture of celebrity: Nicole Brown Simpson would have known that her famous-not-black husband commanded a certain deference from the L.A.P.D. which she, who was white but not yet famous, did not.

"It's just amazing that we in the black community have bought into it," Anita Hill says, with some asperity, and she sees the manufacture of black-male heroes as part of the syndrome. "We continue to create a superclass of individuals who are above the rules." It bewilders her that Simpson "was being honored as someone who was being persecuted for his politics, when he had none," she says. "Not only do we forget about the abuse of his wife but we also forget about the abuse of the community, his walking away from the community." And so Simpson's connection to a smitten black America can be construed as yet another romance, another troubled relationship, another case study in mutual exploitation.

Yet to accept the racial reduction ("WHITES V. BLACKS," as last week's *Newsweek* headline had it) is to miss the fact that the black community itself is riven, and in ways invisible to most whites. I myself was convinced of Simpson's guilt, so convinced that in the middle of the night before the verdict was to be announced I found myself worrying about his prospective sojourn in prison: Would he be brutalized, raped, assaulted? Yes, on sober reflection, such worries over a man's condign punishment seemed senseless, a study in misplaced compassion; but there it was. When the verdict was announced, I was stunned—but, then again, wasn't my own outrage mingled with an unaccountable sense of relief? Anna Deavere Smith says, "I am seeing more than that white people are pissed off and black people are ecstatic. I am seeing the difficulty of that; I am seeing people having difficulty talking about it." And many are weary of what Ishmael Reed calls "zebra journalism, where everything is seen in black-and-white." Davis says, "I have the feeling that the media are in part responsible for the creation of this so-called racial divide—putting all the white people on one side and all the black people on the other side."

Many blacks as well as whites saw the trial's outcome as a grim enactment of Richard Pryor's comic rejoinder "Who are you going to believe—me, or your lying eyes?" "I think if he were innocent he wouldn't have behaved that way," Jamaica Kincaid says of Simpson, taking note of his refusal to testify on his own behalf. "If you are innocent," she believes, "you might want to admit you have done every possible thing in the world—had sex with ten donkeys, twenty mules—but did not do this particular thing." William Julius Wilson says mournfully, "There's something wrong with a system where it's better to be guilty and rich and have good lawyers than to be innocent and poor and have bad ones."

The Simpson verdict was "the ultimate in affirmative action," Amiri Baraka says. "I *know* the son of a bitch did it." For his part, Baraka essentially agrees with Shapiro's rebuke of Cochran: "Cochran is belittling folks. What he's saying is 'Well, the niggers can't understand the question of perjury in the first place. The only thing they can understand is, 'He called you a nigger.' " He alludes to *Ebony's* fixation on "black firsts"—the magazine's spotlight coverage of the first black to do this or that—and fantasizes the appropriate *Ebony* accolade. "They can feature him on the cover as 'The first Negro to kill a white woman and get away with it,' " he offers acidly. Then he imagines Farrakhan introducing him with just that tribute at the Million Man March. Baraka has been writing a play called *Othello, Jr.*, so such themes have been on his mind. The play is still in progress, but he *has* just finished a short poem:

> *Free Mumia!*
> *O.J. did it*
> *And you know it.*

"Trials don't establish absolute truth; that's a theological enterprise," Patricia Williams says. So perhaps it is appropriate that a religious leader, Louis Farrakhan, convened a day of atonement; indeed, some worry that it is all too appropriate, coming at a time when the resurgent right has offered us a long list of sins for which black men must atone. But the crisis of race in America is real enough. And with respect to that crisis a mass mobilization is surely a better fit than a criminal trial. These days, the assignment of blame for black woes increasingly looks like an exercise in scholasticism; and calls for interracial union increasingly look like an exercise in inanity. ("Sorry for the Middle Passage, old chap. I don't know *what* we were thinking." "Hey, man, forget it—and here's your wallet back. No, really, I want you to have it.") The black economist Glenn Loury says, "If I could get a million black men together, I wouldn't march them to Washington, I'd march them into the ghettos."

But because the meanings of the march are so ambiguous, it has become itself a racial Rorschach—a vast ambulatory allegory waiting to happen. The actor and director Sidney Poitier says, "If we go on such a march to say to ourselves and to the rest of America that we want to be counted among America's people, we would like our family structure to be nurtured and strengthened by ourselves and by the society, that's a good point to make." He sees the march as an occasion for the community to say, "Look, we are adrift. Not only is the nation adrift on the question of race—we, too, are adrift. We need to have a sense of purpose and a sense of direction." Maya Angelou, who agreed to address the assembled men, views the event not as a display of male self-affirmation but as a ceremony of penitence: "It's a chance for African-American males to say to African-American females, 'I'm sorry. I am sorry for what I did, and I am sorry for what happened to both of us.' " But different observers will have different interpretations. Mass mobilizations launch a thousand narratives—especially among subscribers to what might be called the "great event" school of history. And yet Farrakhan's recurrent calls for individual accountability consort oddly with the absolution, both juridical and populist, accorded O. J. Simpson. Simpson has been seen as a symbol for many things, but he is not yet a symbol for taking responsibility for one's actions.

All the same, the task for black America is not to get its symbols in shape: Symbolism is one of the few commodities we have in abundance. Meanwhile, De Bois's century-old question "How does it feel to be a problem?" grows in trenchancy with every new bulletin about crime and poverty. And the Simpson trial spurs us to question every-thing except the way that the discourse of crime and punishment has enveloped, and suffocated, the analysis of race and poverty in this country. For the debate over the rights and wrongs of the Simpson verdict has meshed all too well with the manner in which we have long talked about race and social justice. The defendant may be free, but we remain captive to a binary discourse of accusation and counter-accusation, of grievance and countergrievance, of victims and victim-izers. It is a discourse in which O. J. Simpson is a suitable remedy for Rodney King, and reductions in Medicaid are entertained as a suitable remedy for O. J. Simpson—a discourse in which everyone speaks of payback and nobody is paid. The result is that race politics becomes a court of the imagination wherein blacks seek to punish whites for their misdeeds and whites seek to punish blacks for theirs, and an infi-nite regress of score-settling ensues—yet another way in which we are daily becoming meta and meta. And so an empty vessel like O. J. Simpson becomes filled with meaning, and more meaning—more meaning than any of us can bear. No doubt it is a far easier thing to assign blame than to render justice. But if the imagery of the court continues to confine the conversation about race, it really will be a crime.

luis j.
rodriguez
susan
straight

adrienne
rich
gerald
early
russell
leong
leslie
marmon
silko
john
edgar
wideman

luis j. rodríguez

luis j. rodríguez

Luis J. Rodríguez, born in 1954, grew up in Watts and East Los Angeles, the son of Mexican immigrants. He joined his first gang at the age of eleven and by the age of eighteen was a veteran of gang warfare, which had taken the lives of many of his friends. His prose masterpiece, *Always Running*, while chronicling his gang life in L.A., evolves into a story of survival and transcendence. Rodríguez began writing poetry in his early teens. His first book, *Poems Across the Pavement*, won the Poetry Center Book Award from San Francisco State University. In 1991 *The Concrete River* won a PEN West/Josephine Miles Award for Literary Excellence. He received a 1992 Lannan Fellowship in Poetry.

A fierce honesty drives the narrative voice of Luis Rodríguez. His writing in poetry or prose is like a man who has tossed open his doors and windows to capture all the available light. Although never prescriptive, Rodríguez's powerful narratives persuade us that if we do not open to our own truths, and care about those with less opportunity than ourselves, we will only live half lives in an ailing society.

Luis J. Rodríguez lives in Chicago, where he runs Tia Chucha Press, which publishes emerging, socially-conscious poets.

two generations

*"We have the right to lie, but not about
the heart of the matter."*
—Antonin Artaud

Late winter Chicago, early 1991: The once-white snow which fell in December had turned into a dark scum, mixed with ice-melting salt, car oil, and decay. Icicles hung from rooftops and windowsills like the whiskers of old men.

For months, the bone-chilling "hawk" swooped down and forced everyone in the family to squeeze into a one-and-a-half-bedroom apartment in a gray-stone, three-flat building in the Humboldt Park neighborhood.

Inside tensions built up like fever as we crammed around the TV set or kitchen table, the crowding made more intolerable because of heaps of paper, opened file drawers, and shelves packed with books that garnered every section of empty space (a sort of writer's torture chamber). The family included my third wife, Trini; our child, Rubén Joaquín, born in 1988; and my fifteen-year-old son Ramiro (a thirteen-year-old daughter, Andrea, lived with her mother in East Los Angeles).

We hardly ventured outside. Few things were worth heaving on the layers of clothing and the coats, boots, and gloves required to step out the door.

Ramiro had been placed on punishment, but not for an act of disobedience or the usual outburst of teenage anxiety. Ramiro had been on a rapidly declining roller-coaster ride into the world of street-gang

America, not unexpected for this neighborhood, once designated as one of the ten poorest in the country and also known as one of the most gang-infested.

Humboldt Park is a predominantly Puerto Rican community with growing numbers of Mexican immigrants and uprooted blacks and sprinklings of Ukrainians and Poles from previous generations. But along with the greater West Town area it was considered a "changing neighborhood," dotted here and there with rehabs, signs of gentrification, and, for many of us, imminent displacement.

Weeks before, Ramiro had received a ten-day suspension from Roberto Clemente High School, a beleaguered school with a good number of caring personnel, but one which, unfortunately, was an epicenter of gang activity. The suspension came after a school fight which involved a war between "Insanes" and "Maniacs," two factions of the "Folks" ("Folks" are those gangs allied with the Spanish Cobras and Gangster Disciples; the "People" are gangs tied to the Latin Kings and Vice Lords, symbolic of the complicated structures most inner-city gangs had come to establish). There was also an "S.O.S."— a "smash-on-sight"—contract issued on Ramiro. As a result I took him out of Clemente and enrolled him in another school. He lasted less than two weeks before school officials there kicked him out. By then I also had to pick him up from local jails following other fighting incidents—and once from a hospital where I watched a doctor put eleven stitches above his eye.

Following me, Ramiro was a second-generation gang member. My involvement was in the late 1960s and early 1970s in Los Angeles, the so-called gang capital of the country. My teen years were ones of drugs, shootings and beatings, and arrests. I was around when south-central Los Angeles gave birth to the Crips and Bloods. By the time I turned eighteen years old, twenty-five of my friends had been killed by rival gangs, police, drugs, car crashes, and suicides.

If I had barely survived all this—to emerge eventually as a journalist, publisher, critic, and poet—it appeared unlikely my own son would make it. I had to cut his blood line to the street early, before it became too late. I had to begin the long, intense struggle to save his life from the gathering storm of street violence sweeping the country—some twenty years after I sneaked out of my 'hood in the dark of night, hid out in an L.A. housing project and removed myself from the death-fires of *La Vida Loca*.

La Vida Loca or The Crazy Life is what we called the barrio gang experience. This lifestyle originated with the Mexican pachuco gangs of the 1930s and 1940s, and was later re-created with the Cholos. It became the main model and influence for outlaw bikers of the 1950s and 1960s, the L.A. punk/rock scene in the 1970s and 1980s, and the Crips and Bloods of the 1980s and early 1990s. As Leon Bing commented in his 1991 book *Do or Die* (HarperCollins): "It was the *cholo* homeboy who first walked the walk and talked the talk. It was the Mexican-American *pachuco* who initiated the emblematic tattoos, the singing with hands, the writing of legends on walls."

One evening that winter, after Ramiro had come in late following weeks of trouble at school, I gave him an ultimatum. Yelling burst back and forth between the walls of our Humboldt Park flat. Two-year-old Rubén, confused and afraid, hugged my leg as the shouting erupted. In a moment, Ramiro ran out of the house, entering the cold Chicago night without a jacket. I went after him, although by my mid-thirties I had gained enough weight to slow me down considerably. Still I sprinted down the gangway which led to a debris-strewn alley, filled with furniture parts and overturned trash cans. I saw Ramiro's fleeing figure, his breath rising above him in quickly dissipating clouds.

I followed him toward Augusta Boulevard, the main drag of the neighborhood. People yelled out of windows and doorways: "*¿Qué pasa, hombre?*" Others offered information on Ramiro's direction. A father or mother chasing some child down the street is not an unfamiliar sight around here.

A city like Chicago has so many places in which to hide. The gray-and-brown-brick buildings seem to suck people in. Ramiro would make a turn and then vanish, only to pop up again. Appearing and disappearing. He flew over brick walls, scurried down another alley, then veered into a building that swallowed him up and spit him out the other side.

I kept after Ramiro until, unexpectedly, I found him hiding in some bushes. He stepped out, unaware I was to the side of him.

"Ramiro . . . come home," I gently implored, knowing if I pounced on him there would be little hope he'd come back. He sped off again.

"Leave me alone!" he yelled.

As I watched his escape, it was like looking back into a distant time, back to my own youth, when I ran and ran, when I jumped over peeling fences, fleeing *vatos locos*, the police, or my own shadow in some drug-induced hysteria.

I saw Ramiro run off and then saw *my* body entering the mouth of darkness, my breath cutting the frigid flesh of night; it was my voice cracking open the winter sky.

Ramiro was born just prior to my twenty-first birthday. I had been working in a steel mill in Los Angeles. His mother, Camila, not yet nineteen, was an East Los Angeles woman who grew up in one of East L.A.'s roughest barrios: La Gerahty Loma. Yet Camila and her five sisters, with the help of their mother, managed to stave off attempts to pull them into the street life there—even having battles on their front porch with the *locas* who tried to recruit them.

The media likens Los Angeles to a "Beirut by the Beach." For 1991, police cited these statistics: 100,000 gang members, 800 gangs, nearly 600 young people killed. Parts of the city, particularly the public housing projects, have been called "ungovernable." These stats have been used to create a hysteria against black and Latino youth. Police in L.A. have practically instituted martial law in the inner city. Michael Davis, in his book *City of Quartz* (Verso Press, 1991), says that by 1990 the various law enforcement "operations" to destroy gangs (using helicopters, infrared lights, and made-over armored vehicles—not far behind what was used in "Desert Storm") detained or arrested fifty thousand youth, in south-central alone.

The Crazy Life in my youth, although devastating, was only the beginning stages of what I believe is now a consistent and growing genocidal level of destruction predicated on the premise there are marginalized youth with no jobs or future, and therefore expendable.

Camila's brothers weren't spared. One of them became active in Gerahty Loma, a witness to a number of killings himself, and later a heroin addict and a convict. Another brother got jumped and stabbed seven times—but survived. And an older half-brother was killed while trying to exact some revenge one night near the Mexican border.

Later, her nephews from an older sister got involved in the barrio and one of them, known as Shorty, was murdered outside his home at the age of seventeen (but not before he fathered a baby).

When Ramiro was two years old, and his sister only ten months, Camila and I broke up. About seven years later, I moved to Chicago. After being left behind, Ramiro failed miserably in school, although he had been tested as a gifted child. He ran away from home a number of times. Once, when he was about ten years old, he hopped a train from L.A. to Chicago, but police pulled him out of a boxcar before he passed the city limits. When he turned thirteen years old, he came to stay with me. Because of what Camila and I had been through, we tried everything we could to keep him out of the "life," even after we divorced and lived a couple of thousands of miles apart. But often there was too much against us.

In East L.A. and in schools like Chicago's Clemente were some of the nation's highest drop-out rates. Youth employment hovered around 70 percent in the most neglected areas. And what of those who did everything right, got all the good grades, and followed the "rules"? Camila, for example, had been an A student at Garfield High School (site of the 1988 movie *Stand and Deliver*) and was active in school affairs. But after we married, she applied for work and was told she didn't know enough to get a basic nine-to-five office job. She even had to go back to some classes to make up for the lack of schooling she received despite being one of the best students at Garfield! The fact that L.A. schools now give "warranties" only underscores the point.

With little productive to do, drug selling becomes a lucrative means of survival. A ten-year-old in Humboldt Park can make $80 to $100 a day as a lookout for local dealers. The drug trade is business. It's capitalism: cutthroat, profit-motivated, and expedient. Also, the values which drive gangs are linked to the control of markets, in a way similar to what has created borders between nations. In communities with limited resources like Humboldt Park and East L.A., sophisticated survival structures evolved, including gangs, out of the bone and sinew tossed up by this environment.

After Ramiro ran away, he failed to return home for another two weeks. I was so angry at him for leaving, I bought locks to keep him out. I kept a vigil at home to catch him should he sneak in to eat. But then I remembered what I had been through. I recalled how many institutions and people had failed my son—and now he was expected to rise above all this! Soon I spent every night he was gone driving around the streets, talking to the "boys" in their street-corner domains, making daily calls to the police. I placed handwritten notes in the basement which said it was okay for him to come back. I left food for him to get to. Suddenly, every teenage Latino male looked like Ramiro.

With the help of some of his friends, I finally found Ramiro in a run-down barrio hovel and convinced him to come home. He agreed to obtain help in getting through some deep emotional and psychological problems—stemming in large part from an unstable childhood, including abuse he sustained as a kid from his stepfathers, one who was an alcoholic and another who regularly beat him. And I could not remove myself from being struck by the hammerhead of responsibility. A key factor was my relative lack of involvement in Ramiro's life as I became increasingly active in politics and writing.

Although the best way to deal with one's own children is to help construct the conditions that will ensure the free and healthy development of all, it's also true you can't be for all children if you can't be for your own.

By mid-l991, Ramiro had undergone a few months in a psychiatric hospital and various counseling and family sessions that also involved bringing his mother in from L.A. We implemented an educational and employment plan, worked out with school officials, teachers, and social workers (everyone who had dealings with him had to be involved, to get them on "our side" so to speak). I also learned a parent cannot just turn over a child to a school, a court, or hospital without stepping in at various times to ensure his or her best interests are being met. My aim was to help Ramiro get through his teenage years with a sense of empowerment and esteem, with what I call complete literacy: the ability to participate competently and confidently in any level of society one chooses.

There is an aspect of suicide in young people whose options have been cut off. They stand on street corners, flashing hand signs, inviting the bullets. It's either *la torcida* or death: a warrior's path, when even self-preservation is not at stake. And if they murder, the victims are usually the ones who look like them, the ones closest to who they are—the mirror reflections. They murder and they're killing themselves, over and over.

At the same time, individual efforts must be linked with social ones. I tried to get Ramiro to understand the systematic nature of what was happening in the street, which in effect made choices for him before he was born. The thing is, no matter what one does individually, in this setting, dangers keep lurking around every corner.

A couple of examples helped Ramiro see the point. Not long ago, a few of his friends were picked up by police, who drove them around in a squad car. The police took them to a rival gang neighborhood. There they forced Ramiro's friends to spray paint over the graffiti with their own insignias—as rival gang members watched—and then left them there to find their way home. It's an old police practice.

A second incident involved the shooting death of a Dragon, a

Puerto Rican teenager named Efrain, who Ramiro knew. Soon after, we happened to drive through a Latin Kings' territory. The words "Efrain Rots" had been emblazoned on a wall. That night, Ramiro sat alone, intensely quiet, in the backyard, thinking about this for a long time.

Things between us, for now, are being dealt with day by day. Although Ramiro has gained a much more viable perspective on his place in the world, there are choices he has to make "not just once, but every time they come up."

Meanwhile, I've pursued writing this book—after a ten-year lapse. The writing first began when I was fifteen, but the urgency of the present predicament demands it finally see the light of day. This work is an argument for the reorganization of American society—not where a few benefit at the expense of the many, but where everyone has access to decent health care, clothing, food, and housing, based on need, not whether they can afford them. It's an indictment against the use of deadly force, which has been the principal means this society uses against those it cannot accommodate (as I write this, Rodney King's beating by the LAPD continues to play itself out throughout the country, and the *Los Angeles Daily News* in late October 1991 reported that the L.A. County Sheriff's Department had shot fifty-five people since the first of the year—over 50 percent were people of color, and a few were disabled or mentally ill; some of them were unarmed or shot in the back).

Criminality in this country is a class issue. Many of those warehoused in overcrowded prisons can be properly called "criminals of want," those who've been deprived of the basic necessities of life and therefore forced into so-called criminal acts to survive. Many of them just don't have the means to buy their "justice." They are members of a social stratus which includes welfare mothers, housing project residents, immigrant families, the homeless and unemployed. This book is part of their story.

Although the work begins with my family's trek from Mexico when I was a child and touches on our early years in Watts, it primarily covers the period from ages twelve until eighteen when I became active in Las Lomas barrio.

This work is not fiction, yet there are people I don't want hurt by having their names and stories made public. I've changed names and synthesized events and circumstances in keeping with the integrity of a literary, dramatic work, as an artist does in striving for that rare instance when, as a critic once said, "something of beauty collides with something of truth."

The more we know, the more we owe. This is a responsibility I take seriously. My hope in producing this work is that perhaps there's a thread to be found, a pattern or connection, a seed of apprehension herein, which can be of some use, no matter how slight, in helping to end the rising casualty count for the Ramiros of this world, as more and more communities come under the death grip of what we called "The Crazy Life."

JULY 1992

susan straight

new year's eve

What did you do on New Year's Eve? Whatever you do, it's what you're going to be doing the rest of the year—that's what my husband and I always heard when we were growing up. So don't fight or work—party and make love and laugh.

This year, we lay in bed and categorized gunfire. "That sounds like an automatic, a nine-millimeter," my husband said. "That's a thirty-eight." I heard a long chattering that lasted for several minutes. "Uzi."

It's too dangerous to go out. When we were in high school together, we went to house parties and cruised in old cars packed shoulder-to-shoulder with our friends. We talked a lot of smack to people from other neighborhoods, especially after football or basketball games; we tried a couple of times to crash parties.

My teenage neighbors are Jersey City natives, Puerto Rican girls. I asked the two of them last week what they were doing on Friday night. "My mom says we can't go out anymore. They were shooting in the parking lot at the mall and the club," Tanya said.

Last year, two streets over, a fourteen-year-old boy was refused entry into a house party. We used to yell and screech away; he went home, got a shotgun, and fired into the house. I don't recall any desire to annihilate people who didn't want to dance with me. But I'm thirty-one. I'm old.

My husband's thirty-three. People are afraid of him. He's six-four, two hundred forty pounds. Let's put it this way: The last time he had a flat, he walked seven miles home from work. You wouldn't stop to give him a ride. And when he stops to help you with your flat, you're terrified. He's black. He's big. He's a walking lethal weapon. People cross the street, clutch their purses, avert their eyes. He laughs.

I have to send him out into the world every morning, and he works crazy shifts. Sometimes it's before sunrise, and then he stops to get gas in the dark. A nervous attendant steps on the silent alarm and seven black-and-whites surround him, gun barrels aimed. He dangles his hands out the car window. He's been doing this for a long time. I've been with him, hands pressed against a brick wall, the circle of metal close to his ear. Walking down the wrong street is dangerous. A malfunctioning turn signal is dangerous. He never speeds.

And if he works swing, he has to avoid boulevards where gang-bangers cruise, because who knows? Maybe somebody driving a truck like ours said something wrong to someone with a nine-millimeter. He avoids eye contact. If he's twenty minutes late, I'm pacing the grass. He never stops off without telling me.

He works at Juvenile Hall. Last month he got three white kids, twelve-year-olds, who robbed a Pizza Hut delivery man at noon on a Wednesday. They had a nine-millimeter. Their fathers are car dealers. How much money did they think they were going to get at noon? On a Wednesday?

My husband and his colleagues were disgusted. They led the boys into Security, which is always full now. Security is for violent crimes. The county just built a big new wing.

Last summer my daughter was two. In the bathtub one night, she asked me for a beeper. "What?" I said. "All the boys across the street from day care have them," she said.

Two rock houses, dealing in that kind of cocaine, operated for six months across from my husband's godmother's house, where she has run a day-care center for thirty years. Yes, we called the police. It's a bad neighborhood, we were told. At night, gunfire peppered walls and streetlights and the sky so often no one even called the cops. And finally, I wrote a petition. I'm the writer. My relatives got signatures. I delivered the pages to our senator and the newspaper. The rock houses were boarded up: code violations. And the older men in the neighborhood, my father-in-law and godfather, oiled their ancient shotguns. "What's that gonna do with an Uzi?" the younger men said. "If I go, I'ma take a punk with me," the older men answered.

"Great," I said. But though the random shooting persists, no one's been hurt. From that feud. Random shooting always looks small in the newspaper. Two lines. And last month, on a Monday at four, I came from work to pick up my two daughters. Standing in my mother-in-law's yard with friends and cousins, I heard shots, but I didn't move fast enough. They screamed at me to run. I think I was reading a memo from work. I ducked and crawled to the doorknob— that was what I focused on. Inside, I ran to the back room, where we always stay when we hear shots.

It was a twenty-five-caliber pistol. A disowned nephew-by-marriage had stood on the corner, idly making gang hand signals, when the wrong carload of guys passed by. They came back shooting, and he ran behind me. "Was that during the riots?" people from New York asked me. No. It was a regular day.

The helicopter is going over now, as I type. It's looking for criminals. But I just got my two girls to bed, and the clattering blades and silvery spotlight wake them back up. My oldest daughter is three now. She plays with Barbies. She says, "Barbie, run, the cops are going to kill us!"

In the car, I tell her, "The policeman is your friend." I remember those words from our elders. "He helps you." But she sees us stiffen when a patrol car is behind us. My husband checks his seat belt.

"Was that shooting?" she asks. I tell her no, it's the Fourth of July. She likes the sparkly fireworks, but she runs to me when the booming ones sound through the night sky.

adrienne rich

adrienne rich

Adrienne Rich, born in 1929, published her first book of poetry, *A Change of World*, at the age of twenty-two, after winning the Yale Younger Poets Award. She has become one of the twentieth century's most important poets and catalysts for change. Her numerous books of poetry include *Diving into the Wreck*, which won a National Book Award in 1974; *The Will to Change*; *The Dream of a Common Language*; and *Your Native Life, Your Life*.

Adrienne Rich has also published four volumes of prose. Her groundbreaking book of 1976, *Of Women Born: Motherhood as an Experience and Institution*, argues with rigorous intelligence for the value of personal experience in women's lives. In a new introduction for its tenth anniversary, Rich said: "*Of Women Born* was both praised and attacked for what was sometimes seen as its odd-fangled approach: personal testimony mingled with research, and theory which derived from both. But this approach never seemed odd to me in the writing. What still seems odd to me is the absentee author, the writer who lays down speculations, theories, facts, and fantasies, without any personal grounding."

In recent books, Rich has focused on the meaning of being an American, and the idea of citizenry. Her long poem *Atlas of the Difficult World* refers to America's common infatuation with its Gulf War arsenal of "Patriot" missiles. She tells us that "A patriot is not a weapon. A patriot is one who wrestles for the soul of her country."

the distance between language and violence

She's calling from Hartford: another young dark-skinned man has been killed—shot by police in the head while lying on the ground. Her friend, riding the train up from New York, has seen overpass after overpass spray painted: "KKK—Kill Niggers." It's Black History Month.

But this is white history.

White hate crimes, white hate speech. I still try to claim I wasn't brought up to hate. But hate isn't the half of it. I grew up in the vast encircling presumption of whiteness—that primary quality of being which knows itself, its passions, only against an otherness that has to be dehumanized. I grew up in white silence that was utterly obsessional. Race was the theme whatever the topic.

In the case of my kin, the word sprayed on the overpasses was unspeakable, part of a taboo vocabulary. *That* word was the language of "rednecks." My parents said "colored," "Negro," more often "They," even sometimes, in French, *"les autres."*

Such language could dissociate itself from lynching, from violence, from such a thing as hatred.

A poet's education. A white child growing into her powers of language within white discourse. Every day, when she is about five years old, her father sets her a few lines of poetry to copy into a ruled notebook as a handwriting lesson:

A thing of beauty is a joy forever;
Its loveliness increases . . .

Tyger, Tyger, burning bright,
In the forests of the night;
What immortal hand or eye,
Could frame thy fearful symmetry?

She receives a written word in her notebook as grade: "Excellent," "Very good," "Good," "Fair," "Poor." The power of words is enormous; the rhythmic power of verse, rhythm meshed with language, excites her to imitation. Later, she begins reading in the books of poetry from which she copied her lessons. Blake, especially, she loves. She has no idea whether he, or Keats, or any of the poets is alive or dead, or where they wrote from: poetry, for her, is now and here. The "Songs of Innocence" seem both strange and familiar:

When the voices of children are heard on the green
And laughing is heard on the hill,
My heart is at rest within my breast
And everything else is still.

And

My mother bore me in the southern wild,
And I am black, but O! my soul is white;
White as an angel is the English child:
But I am black, as if bereav'd of light.

This poem disturbs her faintly, not because it in any way contradicts the white discourse around her, but because it seems to approach the perilous, forbidden theme of color, the endless undertone of that discourse.

She is not brought up to hate; she is brought up within the circumference of white language and metaphor, a space that looks and feels to her like freedom. Early on, she experiences language, especially poetry, as power: an elemental force that is *with* her, like the wind at her back as she runs across a field.

Only much later she begins to perceive, reluctantly, the relationships of power sketched in her imagination by the language she loves and works in. How hard, against others, that wind can blow.

White child growing into her whiteness. Tin shovel flung by my hand at the dark-skinned woman caring for me, summer 1933, soon after my sister's birth, my mother ill and back in the hospital. A half-effaced, shamed memory of a bleeding cut on her forehead. I am reprimanded, made to say I'm sorry. I have "a temper," for which I'm often punished; but this incident remains vivid while others blur. The distance between language and violence has already shortened. Violence becomes a language. If I flung words along with the shovel, I can't remember them. Then, years later, I do remember. *Negro! Negro!* The polite word becomes epithet, stands in for the evil epithet, the taboo word, the curse.

A white child's anger at her mother's absence, already translated (some kind of knowledge makes this possible) into a racial language. That *They* are to blame for whatever pain is felt.

This is the child we needed and deserved, my mother writes in a notebook when I'm three. My parents require a perfectly developing child, evidence of their intelligence and culture. I'm kept from school, taught at home till the age of nine. My mother, once an aspiring pianist and composer who earned her living as a piano teacher, need not—and must not—work for money after marriage. Within this bubble of class privilege, the child can be educated at home, taught to play Mozart on the piano at four years old. She develops facial tics, eczema in the creases of her elbows and knees, hay fever. She is prohibited confusion: her lessons, accomplishments, must follow a clear trajectory. For her parents she is living proof. A Black woman cleans the apartment, cooks, takes care of the child when the child isn't being "educated."

Mercifully, I had time to imagine, fantasize, play with paper dolls and china figurines, inventing and resolving their fates. The best times were times I was ignored, could talk stories under my breath, loving my improvised world almost as much as I loved reading.

Popular culture entered my life as Shirley Temple, who was exactly my age and wrote a letter in the newspapers telling how her mother fixed spinach for her, with lots of butter. There were paper-doll books of her and the Dionne Quintuplets—five identical girls born to a French-Canadian family—and of the famous dollhouse of the actress Colleen Moore, which contained every luxury conceivable in perfect miniature, including a tiny phonograph that played Gershwin's *Rhapsody in Blue*. I was impressed by Shirley Temple as a little girl my age who had power: She could write a piece for the newspapers and have it printed in her own handwriting. I must have seen her dancing with Bill "Bojangles" Robinson in *The Littlest Rebel*, but I remember her less as a movie star than as a presence, like President Roosevelt, or Lindbergh, whose baby had been stolen; but she was a little girl whose face was everywhere—on glass mugs and in coloring books as well as in the papers.

Other figures peopling my childhood: the faceless, bonneted woman on the Dutch Cleanser can; Aunt Jemima beaming on the pancake box; "Rastus," the smiling Black chef on the Cream of Wheat box; the "Gold Dust Twins" capering black on orange on soap boxes, also in coloring books given as premiums with the soap powder. (The white obsession wasn't silent where advertising logos were concerned.) The Indian chief and the buffalo, "vanished" but preserved on the nickel. Characters in books read aloud: Little Black Sambo, Uncle Remus—with accompanying illustrations. Hiawatha. The Ten Little Indians, soon reduced to none, in the counting-backward rhyme.

In 1939 came the New York World's Fair. Our family, including my paternal grandmother, took the train from Baltimore and stayed two or three nights at the Hotel Pennsylvania in New York, across the street from Pennsylvania Station. We saw the Rockettes at Radio City Music Hall, spent a day in Flushing Meadows at the Fair, with its Trylon and Perisphere of which we had heard so much. We went to Atlantic City for a day, chewed its saltwater taffy, were pushed in wicker chairs along the boardwalk (a favorite tourist ride in Atlantic City in those days—hard to fathom its appeal to a child). My sister and I had our portraits sketched in pastel by a boardwalk artist. Under her picture he wrote, "Dad's Pride," and under mine, "Miss America, 1949."

It was going to be a long way to 1949. In a month war would be declared in Europe; soon the Atlantic Ocean would be full of convoys, submarines, and torpedoes; in Baltimore, we would have blackouts, and air-raid drills at school. I would become part of the first American "teenage" generation, while people my age in Europe were, unbeknownst to me, being transported east in cattle cars, fighting as partisans, living in hiding, sleeping underground in cratered cities. Pearl Harbor would call in the wrath of the United States.

I was keeping a "Line-A-Day" diary and wrote of the World's Fair: "The greatest part was the World of Tomorrow. Men and women of Tomorrow appeared in the sky and sang." Some early version of big-screen vision and sound must have been projected on the dome of the Perisphere, celebrating the World of Tomorrow with its material goods, miracle conveniences, freeways, skyways, aerial transport. No World War II, no Final Solution, no Hiroshima. The men and women of Tomorrow marched with energetic and affirming tread. Whatever they sang, it wasn't the "Internationale"—more like a hymn to American technology and free enterprise. The Depression was still on, the Nazi invasion of Czechoslovakia only a few weeks away. But the World of Tomorrow—capitalist kitsch—inspired a nine-year-old girl, who, decades later, remembers but one other moment from the New York World's Fair of 1939: a glassblower blew, over live fire, a perfect glass pen and nib in translucent blue-green, and handed it over to her to keep, and she did keep it, for many years.

Mercifully, at last, I was sent to school, to discover other, real children; born into other families, other kinds of lives. Not a wide range, at a private school for white girls. Still, a new horizon.

Mercifully, I discovered *Modern Screen*, *Photoplay*, Jack Benny, "Your Hit Parade," Frank Sinatra, "The Romance of Helen Trent," "Road of Life." The war was under way; I learned to swing my hips to "Don't Sit Under the Apple Tree," "Deep in the Heart of Texas," "Mairzy Doats," "Don't Get Around Much Anymore." I loved Walter Pidgeon and the singing of the miners in *How Green Was My Valley*, Irene Dunne in *The White Cliffs of Dover*. I learned to pick out chords for "Smoke Gets in Your Eyes" and "As Time Goes By" on the keyboard devoted to Mozart.

A poet's education. Most of the poetry she will read for many years, when poetry is both sustenance and doorway, is not only written by white men but frames an all-white world; its images and metaphors are not "raceless" but rooted in an apartheid of the imagination. In college, for a seminar in modern American poetry that includes no Black (and almost no women) poets, she reads one of Allen Tate's "Sonnets at Christmas":

> *Ah, Christ, I love you rings to the wild sky*
> *And I must think a little of the past:*
> *When I was ten I told a stinking lie*
> *That got a black boy whipped; but now at last*
> *The going years, caught in an accurate glow,*
> *Reverse like balls englished upon green baize—*
> *Let them return, let the round trumpets blow*
> *The ancient crackle of the Christ's deep gaze.*
> *Deafened and blind, with senses yet unfound,*
> *Am I, untutored to the after-wit*

Of knowledge, knowing a nightmare has no sound;
Therefore with idle hands and head I sit
In late December before the fire's daze
Punished by crimes of which I would be quit.

This girl, this student, this poet is only barely learning that poetry occurs in "periods" and "movements." She is still trying to read the way she always has: In the here and now, what makes you shudder with delight or trouble, what keeps you reading, what's boring? But she's hearing about a southern poetry (she who grew up in the city of Edgar Allan Poe and Sidney Lanier) that calls itself Fugitive, Agrarian. Nothing helps her to connect these literary movements with southern history, with her own history. Tate's sonnet leaps out at her because it breaks, or seems to break, a silence—at very least it seems to point to something under the surface, the unspeakability of which her pulse is tracking as it flickers through the poem. She is studying in New England now, joking about her southern heritage, there are a few African-American students (still known as "Negroes") in her classes, she knows now that "segregation" (a name for the laws she grew up under) and "prejudice" (a vaguer notion) are retrograde; the freshman sister assigned to her by the college is the daughter of a famous international diplomat, later a Nobel laureate: a distinguished Negro. She takes her light-skinned, serious "sister" out for lunches and coffee, is supposed to guide her with sisterly advice. How is she equipped for this, in the presumption of whiteness? Some years later, she hears that this young woman, whose unsmiling ivory face and dark, backstrained hair have become a perplexing memory, is a suicide.

Tate's poem teaches her nothing except the possibility that race can be a guilty burden on white people, leading them to Christmas Eve depression, and (more usefully) that a phrase like "stinking lie" can effectively be inserted in an elegant modern sonnet. Only years later will she learn that the writer of the poem, aristocrat of the world of southern letters, was, at the very least, and as part of his literary politics, a segregationist and supporter of the Ku Klux Klan.

gerald early

the almost last essay on race in america

1. MUCH ADO ABOUT SOMETHING

I was sorely tempted, pressed by a vain foolhardiness and simple exhaustion, to declare, in bold type, this essay to be the last I would ever write on the subject of race, on the subject of blacks, whites, the American race dilemma—however one wishes to categorize that which has been eternally and unendingly categorized. I was given pause in making such a proclamation by the very practical realization that I have a number of projects in the works that necessitate my continuing to say something on this topic or forfeit a fair portion of my income (such as it is). That is what is known in the vernacular as using your mouth to protect your behind, and behinds, being grossly addicted to ease, are fairly indifferent to what boards of comfort are provided as long as the boards are there. Besides, my authority, my expertise on the subject of race arises from such a genuinely existential and amusing source: to wit, having a black skin. Why strive for anything more when I can write from an unassailable position and, like a true self-absorbed American, perform rites of self-therapy and self-improvement at the same time?

Of course, I am provided with a certain comfort, all the more real because it is so perverse, that this preoccupation with racial writing, or writing about race to be more precise, prevents my being able to write the books I really want to write: biographies of Dorothy Sayers and Howard Pyle, cultural criticism on Shirley Temple, Richard Nixon, and Billy Graham. Nothing satisfies an American more than never quite realizing one's potential, although never being an absolute failure, either; it is a great deal like going through life with a chronic but minor illness, like an allergy or a bad back that flares up only when some lifting or exercise is to be done. It is always a bit pleasing to know that one is missing the mark, as it were, in one's career, sacrificing oneself on the altar of opportunism, cultural stereotyping, and lack of resolve, believing, after all, that one can do better, is more gifted (aren't we all?) than the mere hacks we are.

"If you wrote those books," a friend once said to me, "they would only be of interest to the public because a black person wrote them. Blacks would wonder why you are wasting your time and talent writing books that white people could write, and whites would tell you, subtly of course, that you can't write about them as well as a white person can. So, you won't escape race that way."

Perhaps. At any rate, my youngest daughter, Rosalind, approached me a few days after summer vacation started with a new project: getting recognition for dead white male presidents whom nobody has ever heard of. She worked up a mock copy of a newsletter about Rutherford B. Hayes, who has going against him the fact that he withdrew federal troops from the South in 1877, effectively ending Reconstruction, but who also worked for many philanthropic institutions that helped to fund black education. Rosalind felt the first issue of her publication should deal with the wounds he suffered in the Civil War. "Let's not talk about the race stuff," Rosalind said. "People will expect that because we're black."

"Who do you want to do after Hayes?" I asked.

"How about Taft?" she offered. "I think a lot of people are prejudiced against him 'cause he was fat and couldn't get out of a bathtub."

"What about Warren G. Harding?" I countered. "His reputation needs rescuing."

"Nah," she said quickly. "Everybody will think we're doing him 'cause we think he's black." Ah, Harding! His political enemies—and Joel A. Rodgers (great race chronicler)—believed him to have some Negro in his family woodpile. There is something about being black that amounts to a stigma, a taint—in the old days with someone like Harding and before that when "passing" and the "tragic mulatto" were all the rage in black cultural melodrama—that seems virtually impossible to escape. That is the thing about the race dilemma in the United States, the inequity of it all: Whites can take up or put down the concept of race as they wish, having the considerable convenience of being both "particular" and "universal" in one fell swoop; whereas blacks have picked up the race burden, by necessity, from high tragedy to absurd comedy, as a twenty-four-hour exercise in self-realization.

"You can't afford to get too white, Jerry, in your musings," another friend told me. "Some of this detached, ironical meditating on race is cute, shrewd, entertaining, clever. But don't go overboard with it. Otherwise, you'll find yourself cut off from black folk entirely. And you'll be of no use to the white people who find your writings so engaging, if you no longer have access to the community of difference that makes your difference marketable to the other side."

Here, at last, is a brief reflection, inspired by a recent event, in this almost last essay on race in America.

2. ASSIMILATION AND ALL THAT

"Now it is done," wrote sportswriter Red Smith back in 1951. "Now the story ends. And there is no way to tell it. The art of fiction is dead. Reality has strangled invention. Only the utterly impossible, the inexpressibly fantastic, can ever be plausible again." Smith was talking about Bobby Thomson's shocking ninth-inning home run against Ralph Branca and the Brooklyn Dodgers that gave the New York Giants the 1951 National League pennant. It seems appropriate that in the realm of sports we are still capable of being surprised, shocked, unhinged by some unexpected turn in events. Perhaps only in the world of sports does Bergson's statements—life is a perpetual gushing forth of novelties—actually ring true. Or, more precisely, in sports, we feel most keenly the desire for life to be a gushing forth of ardently expressed novelties framed within a rigid world of formal rules and relentless training. Had O. J. Simpson been a famous actor or politician, war hero or banker, would we have been so drawn to his dilemma, so stunned by his downfall?

Some say that they were as shocked by Simpson being accused of murder as they were by the assassination of John F. Kennedy, and perhaps that is all fitting. Those who grew up on Simpson remember the Kennedy assassination, lived through as children, and perhaps we are shocked, in both instances, by such an abrupt and savage squandering, such a cosmic disregard for the heroism of an outsized youth, of such gifts and advantages. It is one of the major ironies of this country that we waste youth even as we revere it. I thought about Red Smith's famous remarks when I, along with millions of others, saw Simpson's Ford Bronco drive down that southern California highway. Only in America could this happen, I thought, because of our love for the symbolism of cars, speed, the open road, the pursuit. Only for a star athlete could we feel this way because athletes are idealizations of youth and success, our cultural hex against death.

All that remains to be said about the O. J. Simpson affair is that one day soon it will come to an end, and we in this country can get on to talking about something that is more worthy of discussion or something about which, as a culture, we are willing to be more honest. There seem to be two deeply troubling aspects about this case.

First, any discussion of race has been scrupulously avoided by most commentators, a sign of how fully assimilated a cultural figure O. J. Simpson is, a nonpolarizing figure who served as such a striking counterpoint in the seventies to the highly racial, intensely politicized Muhammad Ali of the sixties. No one thinks about Simpson's race or the fact that he was interracially married. Americans, generally, must feel relieved by all this, if not a bit proud about the "progress" we have made on the race question. We have quietly congratulated ourselves on our color blindness in an affair—the sexual relationship between a black man and a white woman, his assaults upon her—which historically would have brought out the most bloodthirsty aspects of our national character. And it is progress indeed when we can give a man a trial and even sympathize with his plight instead of lynching him outright as if he were a wild animal, a demon to be exorcised from our land.

The only dissent has come from voices in the African-American community who have not been so willing to let Mr. Simpson go off into that good integrated night. If my brief tour of Washington and New York for my latest book, *Daughters*, is any indication—I spent a good deal of time on black talk radio during the week the Simpson case broke—then black folk, paranoid as ever about the ultimate white conspiracy to bring down high-placed black male achievers and self-conscious as ever about race and their racialness, have come to see this affair in a different light.

"He ain't had no business marrying no white woman," one black woman caller said indignantly. "As soon as these brothers out here get a little money, here they go giving it to the white woman. Sisters ain't good enough for them. They just got to have Miss Ann."

"People got a right to marry who they want to out here," the host replied. "People are free to do what they want when it comes to marriage."

"No, they aren't either," the woman hotly retorted. "Not when you living in a country that's brainwashing you morning, noon, and night about how great the white woman is. A black woman ain't got a chance. Too many weak-minded brothers out here. If race don't mean nothing in this case, how come all the newspapers, magazines, and the TV news is all telling you every two minutes that Nicole Simpson was beautiful and blond and the two went together like meat and potatoes?"

"What I want to know is why brothers getting demonized for all the sex crimes out here," one black male caller said. "First it's Clarence Thomas and sexual harassment, and all the white women feminists get on his case. Then it's Mike Tyson and rape, and all the feminists get on him. Then it's Michael Jackson and the child abuse thing, and everybody gets on him. Now it's O. J. Simpson and wife beating, and all the feminists get on him. How come well-placed black men are rallying points for all the sex crimes in America? I think the white feminists are just as racist as white men, and they find it convenient to demonize black men for sexual misbehavior like these white folk have always done in this country. And ain't nobody gonna tell me anything different. Every time a black man is accused of doing something, you find out it's a damn epidemic. Now, there's an epidemic of wife beating. If the Menendez brothers had been black, there would be a bunch of magazine articles about how parent killing is an epidemic. Black men are always leading the crime wave."

After the show, on my way back to the hotel, a black cabdriver, thin, talkative, perhaps fifty-five or so, turned to me and said, "I guess O. J. just didn't want anybody else to have that pussy. You know, some men get like that about a particular woman. Just can't stand the idea of somebody else getting that pussy even if you ain't getting it anymore. You ever feel that way about a woman? She had some pussy just drive you right out of your right mind. Just couldn't let that woman alone. I did. Woman damn near wrecked my life. You probably saying, 'Simple-minded bastard, goin' crazy over a piece of ass.' But let me tell you that this was no ordinary piece of ass. This was once-in-a-lifetime ass. If you ain't ever felt that way about at least one woman in your life, you been cheated. You have missed"—and he smiled with brown, spaced teeth—"one of life's great agonies. But goin' crazy over that white pussy, well, that's a bad business for a black man publicly. A black man can't lose control over no white woman in that way."

"But don't you see," I responded, "that you're missing the point. Simpson has as much a right as any other person to be obsessed by

any man, woman, whatever. Why should he have a race burden because his obsession was a white woman? And especially when his own
folk are putting the burden on him. That's what the civil rights movement was all about. So that people in this country could love anybody
of age that they wish to love and have equally the privilege to wreck
their lives over their loves, if they are no wiser than to permit that to
happen."

"You an educated man," the cabbie replied, "and I respect that in
anybody, especially a black man, 'cause you gettin' educated ain't been
no easy thing. But you know and I know that when he beat that
woman, if he killed that woman, it ain't no man killed no woman. It's a
black man done killed a white woman and there's four hundred years
of bad history behind that shit. And you don't get rid of four hundred
years of bad history on no humble or by no marches either. O. J.
Simpson make me feel bad as a black man because he beat and maybe
killed that white woman 'cause people be thinking that's just what a
nigger is supposed to do: go ape-shit out of his mind over a white
woman. I don't give a shit if a nigger fucks a million white women as
long as he don't have that white pussy control him in such a way that
he acts the way white people expect him to act and be smirking at his
ass under they sleeve. You hear what I'm sayin'?"

"If Simpson killed that woman, he didn't do it because she was
white," I said, somewhat annoyed by the old cabbie's prattle.

He pulled up in front of my hotel, quietly wrote out my receipt, accepted his payment and tip with an appreciative "thank you," and, as I
was about to shut the door of the cab, said with a cutting, sardonic
edge, "How do you know what Simpson doesn't even know himself?"
And off he drove.

More recently, there were the articles in the July 18 issue of *Jet* that
painted Simpson's ex-wife as a blond bimbo, a floozy, a lousy mother,
a lazy, self-centered woman who was simply an economic drain on
him. (White women want to marry successful black men only for their
money. They don't love them, so many black folk, especially black

women, would like to believe.) Of course, all the quotations were from Simpson's divorce petition, a biased and not-necessarily-accurate source on the state of Simpson's marriage or the character of Nicole Simpson, to say the least, but the magazine's readers, mostly black folk, are hardly likely to consider that in reading the article. This piece is followed by another on Simpson's first marriage, to a woman named Marguerite, an African-American, that suggests that he never abused his first wife. The implication of both articles is obvious: The interracial marriage was a mistake. Simpson married a worthless white woman who used him, brought out the worst in his character, and has ultimately destroyed him. *Jet* is not so much shaping its readers' thinking, however, as it is reflecting the slant its readers want on this case.

There was something about all of this that disturbed me, as if, for many black folk, we could never free ourselves from our race, could never step back from it for one minute to see the world in another way. Or perhaps I was the fool for thinking it worth the effort to try to see the world differently when, after all, no one, white or black, truly expects you to. For the whites, it was the general psychological enfeeblement and welter of neuroses that your color was heir to, the easiest condition for the black to fall prey to; and for the blacks, it was the consciousness of your kith and kin, of the only reality in the world that was worth believing as real, and the hardest level of awareness to achieve because whites fought so hard to discredit, devalue, and disrupt it.

The *Jet* articles suggest an interpretation of the Simpson case that only a largely Christian, millennarian-obsessed people, like African-Americans, could believe, could desire, could rightly and, strangely enough, sensibly want: This is the racial version of the story of the Prodigal Son. Simpson, through his marriage to Nicole Brown, abandoned the race, denied his birthright, lived as a Jew among gentiles. His downfall is an example to all black folk, especially successful black males, about the tragedy of leaving the race, of falling for the symbols of white success, of a misplaced belief in integration, assimilation, of making it in America.

Simpson wrote of his desire for a certain image in his 1970 autobiography, *O.J., The Education of a Rich Rookie*:

> Needless to say, my popularity has also been a key to my financial success. I'm well aware that others have run just as fast and far without ever earning a fraction of the endorsement money I made in the last year. I'm also aware that I have been accused of playing the Establishment game, trying to get important people to like me in order to further my career. That just isn't true. I'm enjoying the money, the big house, the cars; what ghetto kid wouldn't? But I don't feel that I'm being selfish about it. In the long run, I feel that my advances in the business world will shatter a lot of white myths about black athletes— and give some pride and hope to a lot of young blacks. And when I'm finished with the challenges of football, I'm going to take on the challenge of helping black kids in every way I can. I believe that I can do as much for my people in my own way as a Tommie Smith, a Jim Brown, or a Jackie Robinson may choose to do in another way. That's part of the image I want, too.

But the curious thing about Simpson is that he has been, off the field, such an undistinguished presence, despite the fact that he was probably given more advantages and assets than any black athlete of the twentieth century before the coming of Michael Jordan. Perhaps some blacks have been vociferous in seeing the case racially because they have been disappointed, even ashamed, that Simpson, feeling the weight of the presence of Jackie Robinson, Jim Brown, Tommie Smith, feeling the weight of the black athlete in American history, has done so little. It is dismaying to think that Simpson's murder trial may upstage Muhammad Ali's 1967 draft evasion case for future generations of Americans, black and white. The Ali case will remain the most important episode in the history of American jurisprudence. So much more was at stake that was so damn more important with Ali than Simpson. Ali was such a profile in courage.

3.

> *In a society where the rights and potential of women are*
> *constrained, no man can be truly free. He may have power, but he*
> *will not have freedom.*
>
> —MARY ROBINSON, *President of Ireland*

The second troubling aspect of the Simpson case is this: If we have been unable to deal forthrightly with racial issues that confound us in this situation (whites, with some justification, generally eschewing them altogether as an indication of how far we have come, and many blacks, with equal justification, wallowing in them as an indication of how far we have yet to go), we have been even less able to cope with another, far more important, element in this tragedy.

The emphasis on wife beating does not address the major issue here but, through the moral fervor that combines self-righteousness with the insipidness of political reform, clouds everything altogether. (And to use a black man as the major symbol of this wretched abuse is a form of assimilation I'd just as soon do without—those four hundred years the black cabbie spoke of are not without cost for everyone.) This is not to deny that wife beating is a problem but just that it is a symptom of something else.

The major issue here is the sorry state of modern marriage, not as a relationship in power (which is how the politically correct wish to see everything these days, as if this were some truly enlightened view of reality), but as a poignant expression of a bad exchange by people who don't know what love is, to use a phrase. Marriage, as the Simpson case shows, still remains a potentially commercial affair (the great hope of class-jumping or financial betterment), one that many of us still badly botch. What is so depressing about the Simpson marriage is how low an estimate each partner apparently had for the other's humanity, each seeing the other as a trophy, a prize.

What startles about this marriage is how each of these shallow persons with some resources and gifts at their disposal squandered them so shamelessly upon objects that were so self-indulgent and, finally, so worthless. They could see nothing larger than themselves, nor could they see anything large within themselves. What we cannot escape here, but what we do not wish to confront, is how much this marriage is a reflection of our human failings, of our entrapment with ourselves. It is not just a reflection of the patriarchal order or the utter emptiness of male power, but the mundane and numbing debasement of human life in which we so willingly participate. Indeed, marriage in the modern world is nothing more, as many free lovers said at the turn of the century, than a form of enslavement for both the man and the woman. For oppression is not just a political reality but a psychological state, a yearning for love, for less loneliness, for the soulfulness of blood, where, of course, everything is willed by both the oppressor and the victim and where the roles switch back and forth so completely that they simply become moods in a composition, a series of wrangled and deranged aesthetics, a wretched theater.

We might be able to profit from our insistence that Simpson is the assimilated American hero if we can see how his heroism and his manhood and his ex-wife's beauty and their supine love of luxury, our creations, after all, reflect our own paltry ideals of a second-rate, déclassé humanity.

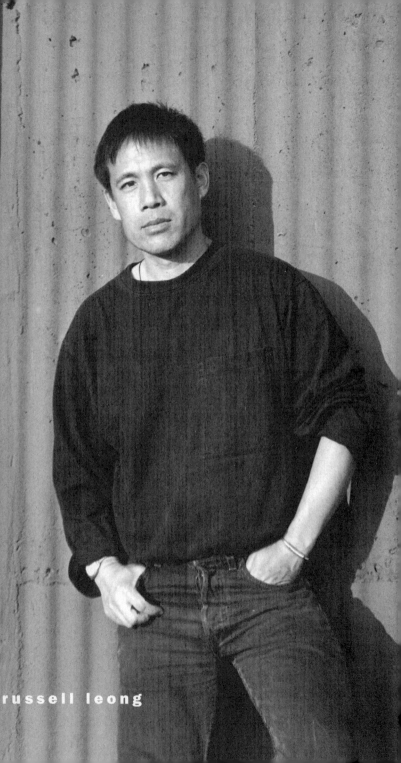
russell leong

russell
leong

Russell Leong was born in 1950 in San Francisco's Chinatown. His volume of poetry *The Country of Dreams and Dust* received a PEN/Josephine Miles Award. His poetry and fiction have been published in *Aiiieeeee!*, *Charlie Chan Is Dead*, the *New England Review*, *The Open Boat*, *Tricycle*, and *ZYZZYVA*. His work was featured recently in the PBS documentary and book *The United States of Poetry*.

Leong is the editor of UCLA's *Amerasia Journal*. He has also edited *Moving the Image: Independent Asian Pacific American Media Arts*, and *Asian American Sexualities: Dimensions of the Gay and Lesbian Experience*.

Russell Leong lives in Los Angeles, where his writing still moves to the mallet of the *mukyi*, the wooden fish drum he heard as a child.

paper houses

Last year, on a whim, I went to the fabled Malibu retreat for an afternoon meditation held by Thich Nhat Hanh, the Vietnamese Buddhist teacher and monk. I told my lover, Jandro, who was driving a Toyota: let me count the number of BMWs and Volvos in the parking lot and I will tell you the composition of the audience. I was skeptical, even cynical as a new Buddhist, but Jandro, being Catholic, let out a big laugh. "Incense or censer—everything looks the same in all that smoke and mumbling!"

We were not the first in the dusty parking lot. A convoy of pastel-colored BMWs, Mazda Miatas, and other imports had preceded us. Couples walked ahead. They were mainly white, with a few mixed white/Asian couples—average age, thirty-eight. The men were mostly blond Nordic types: long-sleeved white cotton or taupe linen shirts rolled back to the elbows, thin expensive watches, tan slacks, and Birkenstock sandals. The Asian American females—Japanese and Chinese—were lean and toned with shiny black hair cascading over their gauzy Indian tunics and tight body leggings. No obvious makeup over their glowing New Age complexions. The half-dozen African-Americans that attended were black males accompanied by white females.

Jandro and I ran into Pama, a Thai friend of mine. The three of us made our way to the grassy knoll and set down our blankets, pillows, and jackets. Clusters of people around us were already munching on granola bars or swilling bottled water. Many were wearing crystal *malas* or sandalwood rosaries around their necks along with New Age healing gems of amethyst, rutilated quartz or topaz dangling on black leather cords.

We had forgotten about preparing food and had bought a large bag of barbecued potato chips, carbonated drinks, and hot dogs at a roadside stand. As we opened our paper bags the people around us began to stare. Others had brought wholesome vegetarian dishes in plastic containers—tofu and grains in assorted forms, cut apples and carrots, and fruit drinks. Here we were, perhaps the only Asian threesome out of three hundred people, eating the most processed food. Pama stared back at them, but soon embarrassed, she slipped the greasy hot dog out of the bun and ate the bread and relish alone. Jandro and I thought to hell with the vegetarian voyeurs and noisily chomped down the rest of the hot dogs and salty orange-dyed chips.

The meditation retreat and lecture began when French and American monks and nuns wearing traditional gray Vietnamese garb took their places around the dais. The French were from Plum Village, the monastery Thich Nhat Hanh had established in France to do his work outside of Viet Nam. The monks and nuns gave a pitch for supporting the work of Plum Village, and then they spoke of the significance of Thich Nhat Hanh's worldwide efforts for peace. (He was nominated for a Nobel prize.) They seemed sincere, yet obviously they had spoken these sentences many times before. After a sitting meditation led by the French nun, Thich Nhat Hanh was introduced by an American male aide. He was a slight, smiling man in a brown robe who appeared direct in manner and unencumbered by his fame or retinue of French and American devotees.

Thich Nhat Hanh began to speak. I remembered only one thing that he said out of that hour: his story of flower and compost. He said that many admire the beauty and fragrance that emanate from flowers. Yet flowers by their nature decay finally: leaf and stamen, filament and anther, pistil and petal lose moisture, crumple and fall to the ground. I glanced at the nape of Jandro's smooth neck, imagining my hand caressing it. Jandro loved flowers, buying them, arranging them, bringing them as gifts to others. Listening to the monk at that time, I had not yet experienced that family, friends or lovers could also flourish, wither, and die. I could not know then that Jandro would leave this world, and me, a few weeks later.

Perhaps it is not surprising that I was drawn to Thich Nhat Hanh, because he was a Vietnamese. Viet Nam had figured strangely in my life as a young man—in the form of Tet, which is the Vietnamese name for the lunar New Year celebration, and which was also the Vietnamese Communist Offensive during the war a quarter of a century ago. I remember, as an American college student, protesting the Vietnam war, because I could not understand killing women and men who looked exactly like my own relatives. But even before Tet and Vietnam, as a youth in San Francisco's Chinatown, I had found myself locked in conflict.

I remember the smell of that day clearly, as pungent as the sun on the asphalt of the basketball court beside the Chinatown alley a few blocks from my family's apartment. As the basketball bounced and landed outside of the fence, I ran to retrieve it and looked up. From the alley, I could see TV antennae and United States and Chinese flags at the corners of the painted balconies unfurling in the breeze.

My white T-shirt was damp with sweat. I loved the body I inherited, the stockiness, muscular legs, and even the large forehead over my darting black eyes. My parents, who worked hard, believed that boys like me who fought right, won at cards, and played fair could fend for themselves. Sisters were another act altogether.

We played in the Presbyterian church courtyard, because in this Asian barrio of four-story walk-ups and small shops, open space was at a premium. Some of us believed in the Father, the Son, and Holy Ghost. Others came just for the space, the friendship, or to check out the girls who came on Sunday for the morning worship. We were second or third generation offspring of working-class Chinatown families descended from Cantonese peasants in Pearl River Delta.

The head of this church was a burly American reverend of Germanic descent, who was a "father" to us, especially the boys. He followed a long line of "Jesus men"—the Reverends William Speer, Otis Gibson, Ira Condit—who had come to Chinatown a century before to teach "heathens" how to pray. For these white missionaries, many of whom were previously stationed in Shanghai, Ningbo, and Canton, the Chinatowns of America were the last Chinese settlements left to conquer. Churches and mission houses duly dotted every third block of my neighborhood: Baptist, Congregational, Catholic, Adventist, Presbyterian, and the True Sunshine Mission.

The reverend ruled his Chinatown roost in a baritone voice. He had a special way of explaining the variations of love to us with Greek terms: *philia, agape, eros.* He'd take us into his office, a wood-paneled inner sanctum lined with bookshelves and knickknacks, and explain doctrine and desire to us patiently. There were stories of fishermen who dropped their nets on the sand to follow Jesus. Fallen women picked up their lives and children again after meeting him. Monkeys and goats, tigers and donkeys in pairs, gingerly stepped onto the giant wooden ark fearing the violent sea beneath them. Being saved, in essence, was a matter of faith and grace that could only be accepted, not earned.

After basketball that day he called me into his office. He whispered *agape* in my ear. It was not his paternal smile or familiar words that disturbed me this time. It was another feeling that I could not name. Suddenly I felt his body—twice as wide and whiter than my real Chinese father—pressed against mine.

His litany worked its way slowly under my skin, soft shrapnel designed for a war I could not win.

"*How doth move a missionary's hand?*"

"Save me with your hands on my chest and legs. Promise not to tell in the name of him who died to save us all."

Were these my words or his?

"Who moves inside me, plucks ribs, forks intestines, enters esophagus, takes tongue?"

"What is a mercenary's hand doing here?"

I grasped the fingers of his hand.

"Where is the shame, what's in a name?"

"What's this evil game?"

My body tailspun like a basketball out of court. I cried foul. The invocation continued. . . .

Flesh versus spirit.

Age versus Youth.

Christian versus Pagan.

Occident versus the Orient.

Colonizer versus the Colonized.

No one could sense my fear behind the mashing of mah-jongg tiles and the buzz of sewing machines in the Chinatown alley. The litany both infuriated and intoxicated me. Mekong machetes sliced their way through bamboo. My legs ran of their own accord, but without a map I was lost. Under his irreverent hands my body slipped.

My T-shirt was sweaty and dirty. Even after I showered and washed the shirt, I could not rid myself of the nameless love and hatred that rose and stuck in my throat. I was estranged from the person I once was. Condemned to silence by the Father, Son, and Holy Ghost, I never said a word to my brother, my parents or friends. Like a chipped Chinatown roof tile unloosened, I fell from the eaves to the ground.

Ornamental figurines graced curio shops in the form of plastic mock-ivory statues of Confucius, Buddha, or Kwan-Yin—goddess of mercy. None of them would lift a hand to save me, an ordinary boy of no consequence. They were one and the same to me—interchangeable icons and images that could be bought, sold, used to decorate home altars, the top of television sets or the mantels of cramped Chinatown apartments. If Christianity betrayed my generation, Buddhism was no less alien to my nature. Buddhism was something that only white poets went to Japan or China to do. They grew beards, wore cotton robes and sandals, and made pilgrimages to Nara and Nepal between bouts of the drugs and sex of the seventies. They had no relation to me. For the most part, they regarded Asians like myself who were born in the Americas as inauthentic and immaterial. Our complex history in this country contradicted all their spiritual or aesthetic notions of orientalness.

The middle-class Mahayana Buddhist temples in Chinatown were filled with slick gold icons, red carpets, and well-dressed Asian Americans who attended services on Sundays. I sometimes visited our family association temple, with its lacquered gilt statues of Kwan-Kung, the warrior-guardian of borders and of the seas. The clicking of joss sticks and the sweetish burnt smell of incense in front of ancestral tablets on the wall hooked me in their narcotic way. But whatever moved through me was as intangible as smoke. When I left Chinatown, l did not want any more to do with religion or Asia.

During the next two decades smoke and sex obscured my life. I drifted, craving the dusky embraces of women and men. I steeped myself in alcohol, and believed, wrongly, that through another's love or loneness, I could be desired or diminished. One day desired, the next day abandoned. New York, Seattle, Taipei, Hong Kong, Naha, Tokyo, Kyoto, Los Angeles. Streets meshed and merged in five languages, then lost me again. I wandered, searching desperately for an identity and a home more hospitable than the one I had left.

In these countries so foreign to my upbringing, I gravitated to temples or gardens. Outside of Kyoto once, I was standing alone with the old granite stones in the garden at a small Zen temple, the Ohara. I realized the temple was closing for the day. Even the brown-robed monks had overlooked my silent presence, and they smiled when they discovered they had almost locked me in for the might. Maybe I should have stayed there then—joined the ancient noble family of stones—and never left. I even now remember that stillness which was not entirely empty. The dusk was filled with the summer noises of shifting branches and evening doves.

Later, and further south along the archipelago, Formosa emerged like a green turtle from the sea. Taipei, its capital, was still under martial law. No matter, I was a U.S. citizen, invincible, like all arrogant, young Americans those days. Like the Chinese and the Japanese and the French in Indochina before me, I was but the latest American colonizer of native brown bodies. One evening I remember climbing up the bamboo scaffolding of an unfinished three-story brick building with a friend. The floors were piled with dust and debris, and there were no stairways connecting the floors yet, just bluish pockets of air. We abandoned ourselves to lust, our feet and slim arms dangling over the edges of darkness. The buzzing of cicadas covered our breathing. Afterwards, we climbed down the scaffolding into that Asian city alive with streets, stairs, and signs that led home. But not to mine. There was "no place like home." Anyway, I never wanted to go home again.

I found love in other places: in alleyways, between palm trees at dusk, in barely furnished rooms, on worn floors, and tatami mats. Sometimes I could not tell the sex of my companions, under their powder and paint, until I pressed myself against their legs. I would walk toward or away from people. Other times motorbikes and their drivers would pick me off the streets and carry me to shabby alcoves in pre–World War II Japanese houses. The mama-san would leave a bucket of cold water, soap, brush, and towel for customers. I would wash and lay naked on the wooden pallet and close my eyes until I felt a stranger's breath on mine.

Some days I would take the bus. On Hsinyi Bus No. 10, I would reach the old Taiwanese section of the city, Yuan Wan, where preserved serpents in glass apothecary jars lined the storefronts of herbalists. Working girls in Japanese wooden and paper houses vied for my money and happiness.

Alongside the bus, Mormon missionaries pedaled on their bicycles, their polyester shirts soured by their large pink bodies, damp with the sweat of faith. As part of their missionary training they had to spend a year or two in a foreign country, in Asia, Africa, or Latin America. They, and the Seventh Day Adventists, competed for the island's brown souls: Taiwan mountain aborigines, innocent country folk, unrepentant bar girls. For a hundred years, as precise as German clockwork, Western soldiers and missionaries seemed to follow one another in war to Manila, Saigon, Seoul, Taipei.

In the late afternoon before the dusk cooled the streets, outside some of the older Japanese houses young girls of no more than fifteen or sixteen would dust the cobblestoned alleys clean, preparing for evening. After dusk fell, many of these same girls would smear their lips red and anoint their cheeks with rouge, and in their thin, cheap cotton dresses pull and tug at the shirt sleeves of any local man who passed through the alleys, urged on by their mama-san who took most of their meager tips. The brothel madame was usually a middle-aged, heavyset woman in a floral print dress, a brightly made-up apparition who cursed at her indentured girls.

One time, I had gone up with a young woman to her reed-matted cubicle, lit by a single bulb. She dipped a white hand towel in a tin basin filled with an astringent mixture of water and vinegar, and told me to pull down my pants. I did, and she cleaned my body with the towel before she pulled up her blouse and placed my hand on her small breasts the size of half-tangerines. I tried to kiss them, but I could not get excited by her naked body. Not because of her sex, but because of her age. She looked away from me without smiling. I apologized, hurriedly put on my clothes and left ten dollars on the worn mat.

Anxiously, I paced the cobblestoned streets. I was a character in a film rewinding upon itself over and over again. Yet, I could not escape those slender white arms that tugged and pulled at my short-sleeved shirt, at my chest and waist. Painted faces were the ghosts of children entangled in their bondage. They laughed at me in disdain when I ignored their pleas and the harsher cries of the older women who owned their bodies.

I found myself stumbling into a small side-street doorway, partly to escape them. It turned out to be a shelter for sailors and seafarers, to Tien Hou, goddess of sailors and protector of the seas. I fell, my knees scraping the worn brick floor of the temple. Tears began to blur my vision. I was no different than those teenage prostitutes. They also had learned to perform acts of love against their feelings.

I, too, was floating on the sea of desire with no sign of harbor. When would I return to myself? Where was my community? In Asia? In America?

As a young man in Asia, I could support myself easily in the company of older men or women. Only after I had run out of money and love and was no longer as desirable, did I return to the United States. I found odd jobs here and there: in a radio station, as a shipping clerk, newspaper assistant, and so forth. So I ended up here, in the City of Angels, as a middle-aged man, forty-four in fact. Old ways of living stayed with me, though with a twist; now I inexplicably sought out the company of much younger men, like Jandro.

Such desires diluted my prayers to Buddha, who had entered my life relatively late. It was around the time of the L.A. riots, driving down the Interstate 5 freeway. The sky was smoky from days and nights of bonfires and rampage. I sought refuge in a Vietnamese Buddhist temple that a friend had introduced me to in Westminster, called "Little Saigon" by the locals. There the monk seemed to understand my wordless despair, not only at the state of the city, but at the state of my self-destructive life. The burning flames, the temple monk told me, could lead to both rain and renewal. He told me to look at the world and myself, clearly, without judgment.

Once home, in the mirror I literally examined my body. No longer lean or agile, it was flaccid like that of the nocturnal madams whom I had encountered in red-lit alleyways years ago. I ran my hands over my shoulders, chest, belly, cock, and thighs. Sweat seeped from my skin. The trapped, stale smells of vinegar, sweat, and sex unfolded in the folds of memory. I reached for my bottle of vodka. It was already emptied.

I recalled the pummeling of the small hands of nameless girls and boys whose bodies were sold by others. With the palm of my hand I struck my face, the stinging bringing warmth suddenly back. But their bruises remained hidden within me, buried beneath the skin's surface.

At least with this body, older and tougher now, I could shield each face and hand from further pain. Even the pain of a lover's death.

For shortly after the Malibu retreat that Jandro and I had both attended, he died unexpectedly, followed by the brush fires and the earthquake. It was as if the moment I turned my face away, he, the mountains, and earth changed into dust.

I returned to the temple I had fled to during the L.A. riots. The monk allowed me to have a forty-nine-day mourning service for Jandro. The forty-ninth day was the Buddhist day of reckoning for the soul of one who has died. At dusk I drove for an hour in the rain to meet his family at the temple. His mother had brought tropical orchids and incense for the altar, a three-foot cardboard and papier-mâché replica of a two-storied house, and square packets of facsimile gold and silver money to burn, as some Chinese from the old country still did. Two of the temple women took the paper items to the patio and set them ablaze with a cigarette lighter.

"Jandro will be richer in his next life," his mother assured herself, and me. But no words came to my mouth. I looked into the darkness and light. Smoke, ashes, and darkness engulfed the space. A single, lime green orchid danced against the orange flames, separated by the thin wall of patio glass. I felt suspended in the shadow and embrace of opposing energies. Pain, pleasure, and prayer melded in that blazing transformation.

All homes in my life have now vanished: paper windows and walls gone up entirely in smoke. A return to home or childhood unsullied by loss and experience was no longer possible. Home was no longer origins, family, or friends. Neither was home the transient refuge of another's embrace or the strong arm of religious belief. I glanced down at my two bare hands. Brown skin held intact the veins, bones, and blood. I would let go of the past. I would no longer crave the future. I would live in this moment.

leslie marmon silko

leslie marmon silko

Leslie Marmon Silko was born in Albuquerque in 1948, of mixed ancestry—Laguna Pueblo, Mexican, and white. She grew up in the Laguna Pueblo Reservation, received a B.A. from the University of New Mexico, and attended law school.

Silko's books include the novels *Ceremony* and *Almanac of the Dead*, a collection of poetry, *Laguna Woman*, and a short-story collection, *The Storyteller*.

She has received grants from the National Endowment for the Arts and the MacArthur Foundation.

Silko's novels, particularly *Ceremony*, have become essential books for many of her readers and are reread with fresh devotion. Of her latest novel William Kittredge said, "Leslie Silko lights up the incipient chickenyard craziness of our culture with fierce intelligence, indignation, and occasional compassion. *Almanac of the Dead* is electrifying, tough to swallow, and likely to be one of our necessary books for a long time."

Leslie Marmon Silko lives in Tucson, Arizona.

fences against freedom

As a person of mixed ancestry, I have always been very sensitive to the prevailing attitudes toward people of color. I remember a time around 1965, when the term "race" was nearly replaced with the term "ancestry" on government forms and applications. For a short time questions about one's ancestry and religion were even deleted from paperwork. During this time, concerted efforts were made by public officials and media people to use the term "ancestry" instead of "race." Geneticists had scientific evidence that there is only one race, the human race; there is only one species to which all people belong: Homo sapiens. This period of conscientious education of the public to eradicate misinformation about "race" grew out of the civil rights movement of the 1950s and from key decisions from the U.S. Supreme Court. Presidents Kennedy and Johnson spoke explicitly about the blot on the honor of the United States made by centuries of prejudice; even the U.S. Congress, with the exception of a few senators and congressmen from southern states, joined them in asserting equality for all human beings.

In 1967, I chose race as my topic for a paper in one of my college honors seminars. I had taken two semesters of anthropology in my freshman year, and I already knew that "race" had been a hot topic among the physical anthropologists for decades. I understood that the "one race, human race" theorists like Ashley Montague had finally assembled incontrovertible biological proof which had swept away the nineteenth-century theories of distinct "races." But I wanted to see exactly how this shift had come about because I knew that many people still were under the influence of nineteenth-century notions concerning race.

I went to the University of New Mexico library and checked out all the books I could find on the topic of "race." As a person of mixed ancestry, I could not afford to take my anthropology professor or Ashley Montague's word for it. Segregationists implied that liberals had seized power on campuses and that to mollify blacks and other "racial" minorities these liberals had concocted false data to prove human equality. My parents and the people of the Laguna Pueblo community who raised me taught me that we are all one family—all the offspring of Mother Earth—and no one is better or worse according to skin color or origin. My whole life I had believed this, but now I had to test what I had been taught as a child because I had also been taught that the truth matters more than anything, even more than personal comfort, more than one's own vanity. It was possible that my parents and the people at home, along with people like Ashley Montague, had deluded themselves just as the segregationists had alleged. I was determined to know the truth even if the truth was unpleasant.

I don't remember all the books I read, but I do remember that Carleton Coon was the name of the leading physical anthropologist whose books and articles argued the "racial superiority" of some "races" over others. I wondered then if Mr. Coon's vehemence about the superiority of the white race had anything to do with his name, which I knew was a common slur used against African-Americans. Had the other children teased him about his name in the schoolyard? Was that why Coon had endured censure by his peers to persist in his "race" research in physical anthropology long after the Nuremberg trials?

I once read an article whose author stated that racism is the only form of mental illness that is communicable. Clever but not entirely true. Racism in the United States is learned by us beginning at birth.

As a person of mixed ancestry growing up in the United States in the late 1950s, I knew all of the cruel epithets that might be hurled at others; the knowledge was a sort of solace that I was not alone in my feelings of unease, of not quite belonging to the group that clearly mattered most in the United States.

Human beings need to feel as if they "belong"; I learned from my father to feel comfortable and happy alone in the mesas and hills around Laguna. It was not so easy for me to learn where we Marmons belonged, but gradually I understood that we of mixed ancestry belonged on the outer edge of the circle between the world of the Pueblo and the outside world. The Laguna people were open and accepted children of mixed ancestry because appearance was secondary to behavior. For the generation of my great-grandmother and earlier generations, anyone who had not been born in the community was a stranger, regardless of skin color. Strangers were not judged by their appearances—which could deceive—but by their behavior. The old-time people took their time to become acquainted with a person before they made a judgment. The old-time people were very secure in themselves and their identity; and thus they were able to appreciate differences and to even marvel at personal idiosyncrasies so long as no one and nothing was being harmed.

The cosmology of the Pueblo people is all-inclusive; long before the arrival of the Spaniards in the Americas, the Pueblo and other indigenous communities knew that the Mother Creator had many children in faraway places. The ancient stories include all people of the Earth, so when the Spaniards marched into Laguna in 1540, the inclination still was to include rather than to exclude the strangers even though the people had heard frightening stories and rumors about the white men. My great-grandmother and the people of her generation were always very curious and took delight in learning odd facts and strange but true stories. The old-time people believed that we must keep learning as much as we can all of our lives. So the people set out to learn if there was anything at all *good* in these strangers, because they had never met any humans who were completely evil. Sure enough, it was true with these strangers, too; some of them had evil hearts, but many were good human beings.

Similarly, when my great-grandfather, a white man, married into the Anaya family, he was adopted into the community by his wife's family and clans. There always had been political factions among these families and clans, and by his marriage, my great-grandfather became a part of the political intrigues at Laguna. Some accounts by anthropologists attempt to portray my great-grandfather and his brother as instigators or meddlers, but the anthropologists have over-estimated their importance and their tenuous position in the Pueblo. Naturally, the factions into which the Marmon brothers had married incorporated these new "sons" into their ongoing intrigues and machinations. But the anthropologists who would portray the Marmon brothers as dictators fool themselves about the power of white men in a pueblo. The minute the Marmon brothers crossed over the line, they would have been killed.

Indeed, people at Laguna remember my great-grandfather as a gentle, quiet man, while my beloved Grandma A'mooh is remembered as a stern, formidable woman who ran the show. She was also a Presbyterian. Her family, the Anayas, had kept cattle and sheep for a long time, and I imagine that way back in the past, an ancestor of hers had been curious about the odd animals the strangers brought and decided to give them a try.

I was fortunate to be reared by my great-grandmother and others of her generation. They always took an interest in us children and they were always delighted to answer our questions and to tell us stories about the old days. Although there were very few children of mixed ancestry in those days, the old folks did not seem to notice. But I could sense a difference from younger people, the generation that had gone to the First World War. On rare occasions, I could sense an anger which my appearance stirred in them, although I sensed that the anger was not aimed at me personally. My appearance reminded them of the outside world where racism was thriving.

I learned about racism firsthand from the Marmon family. My great-grandfather endured the epithet "Squaw Man." Once when he and two of his young sons (my grandpa Hank and his brother, Frank) walked through the lobby of Albuquerque's only hotel to reach the cafe inside, the hotel manager stopped my great-grandfather. He told my great-grandfather that he was welcome to walk through the lobby, but when he had "Indians" with him, he should use the back door. My great-grandfather informed him that the "Indians" were his sons and then he left, and never went into the hotel again.

There were branches of the Marmon family which, although Laguna, still felt they were better than the rest of us Marmons and the rest of the Lagunas as well. Grandpa Hank's sister, Aunt Esther, was beautiful and vain and light-skinned; she boarded at the Sherman Institute in Riverside, California, where my grandfather and other Indian students were taught trades. But Aunt Esther did not get along with the other Indian girls; she refused to speak to them or to have anything to do with them. So she was allowed to attend a Riverside girls school with white girls. My grandfather, who had a broad nose and face and "looked Indian," told the counselor at Sherman that he wanted to become an automobile designer. He was told by the school guidance counselor that Indians weren't able to design automobiles; they taught him to be a store clerk.

I learned about racism firsthand when I started school. We were punished if we spoke the Laguna language once we crossed onto the school grounds. Every fall, all of us were lined up and herded like cattle to the girls' and boys' bathrooms where our heads were drenched with smelly insecticide regardless of whether we had lice or not. We were vaccinated in both arms without regard to our individual immunization records.

But what I remember most dearly are the white tourists who used to come to the schoolyard to take our pictures. They would give us kids each a nickel, so naturally when we saw tourists get out of their cars with cameras, we all wanted to get in the picture. Then one day when I was older, in the third grade, white tourists came with cameras. All of my playmates started to bunch together to fit in the picture, and I was right there with them, maneuvering myself into the group, when I saw the tourist look at me with a particular expression.

I knew instantly he did not want me to be in the picture; I stayed close to my playmates hoping that I had misread the man's face. But the tourists motioned for me to move away to one side, out of his picture. I remember my playmates looked puzzled, but I knew why the man did not want me in his picture: I looked different from my playmates. I was part white and he didn't want me to spoil his snapshots of "Indians." After that incident, the arrival of tourists with cameras at our school filled me with anxiety. I would stand back and watch the expressions on the tourists' faces before trying to join my playmates in the picture. Most times the tourists were kindly and did not seem to notice my difference, and they would motion for me to join my classmates; but now and then there were tourists who looked relieved that I did not try to join in the group picture.

Racism is a constant factor in the United States; it is always in the picture even if it only forms the background. Now, as the condition of the U.S. economy continues to deteriorate and the people grow restive with the U.S. Congress and the president, the tactics of party politicians sink deeper in corruption. Racism is now a trump card, to be played again and again shamelessly by both major political parties. The U.S. government applications that had used the term "ancestry" disappeared; the fiction of "the races" has been reestablished. Soon after Nixon's election the changes began, and racism became a key component once more in the U.S. political arena. The Republican party found the issue of race to be extremely powerful, so the Democrats, desperate for power, have also begun to pander racism to the U.S. electorate.

Fortunately, the people of the United States are far better human beings than the greedy elected officials who allegedly represent them in Congress and the White House. The elected officials of both parties presently are trying to whip up hysteria over immigration policy in the most blatantly racist manner. Politicians and media people talk about the "illegal aliens" to dehumanize and demonize undocumented immigrants who are for the most part people of color. The "cold war" with the Communist world is over, and now the military defense contractors need to create a new bogeyman to justify U.S. defense spending. The U.S.-Mexico border is fast becoming a militarized zone. The army and marine units from all over the United States come to southern Arizona to participate in "training exercises" along the border.

When I was growing up, U.S. politicians called Russia an "Iron Curtain" country, which implied terrible shame. As I got older I learned that there wasn't really a curtain made of iron around the Soviet Union; I was later disappointed to learn that the wall in Berlin was made of concrete, not iron. Now the U.S. government is building a steel wall twelve feet high which eventually will span the entire length of the Mexican border. The steel wall already spans four-mile sections of the border at Mexicali and Naco; and at Nogales, sixty miles south of Tucson, the steel wall is under construction.

Immigration and Naturalization Services, or the Border Patrol, has greatly expanded its manpower and checkpoint stations. Now when you drive down Interstate 10 toward El Paso, you will find a check station. When you drive north from Las Cruces up I-25 about ten miles north of Truth or Consequences, all interstate highway traffic is diverted off the highway into an INS checkpoint. I was detained at that checkpoint in December 1991 on my way from Tucson to Albuquerque for a book signing of my novel *Almanac of the Dead*. My companion and I were detained despite the fact that we showed the Border Patrol our Arizona driver's licenses. Two men from California, both Chicanos, were being detained at the same time, despite the fact that they, too, presented I.D. and spoke English without the thick Texas accents of the Border Patrolmen. While we were detained, we watched as other vehicles were waved through the checkpoint. The occupants of those vehicles were white. It was quite clear that my appearance—my skin color—was the reason for the detention.

The Border Patrol exercises a power that no highway patrol or county sheriff possesses: The Border Patrol can detain anyone they wish for no reason at all. A policeman or sheriff needs to have some shred of probable cause, but not the Border Patrol. In fact, they stop people with Indio-Hispanic characteristics, and they target cars in which white people travel with brown people. Recent reports of illegal immigration by people of Asian ancestry mean that the Border Patrol now routinely detains anyone who looks Asian. Once you have been stopped at a Border Patrol checkpoint, you are under the control of the Border Patrol agent; the refusal to obey any order by the Border Patrol agent means you have broken the law and may be arrested for failure to obey a federal officer. Once the car is stopped, they ask you to step out of the car; then they ask you to open the trunk. If you ask them why or request a search warrant, they inform you that it will take them three or four hours to obtain a search warrant. On this particular day I was due in Albuquerque, and I did not have the four hours to spare. So I opened my car trunk, but not without using my right to free speech to tell them what I thought of them and their police state procedures. "You are not wanted here," I shouted at them, and they seemed astonished. "Only a few years ago we used to be able to move freely within our own country," I said. "This is our home. Take all this back where you came from. You are not wanted here."

The interstate highways, which once symbolized our freedom to travel without the government's interference, are diverted; barriers are erected across the highway and all traffic is funneled off the highway and into Border Patrol checkpoint areas. Motorists are questioned about where they are coming from, and where they are going, and what their business is. If one declines to answer any of the questions, one is detained for hours until a search warrant is obtained for the car, and for your "person." They make it very clear that if you "force" them to get a search warrant, they will strip-search your body as well as your car and luggage.

Scarcely a year later, my friend and I were driving south from Albuquerque, returning to Tucson after a paperback book promotion. There are no Border Patrol detention areas on the southbound lanes of I-25, so I settled back and went to sleep while Gus drove. I awakened when I felt the car slowing to a stop. It was nearly midnight on New Mexico State Road 26, a dark, lonely stretch of two-lane highway between Hatch and Deming. When I sat up, I saw the headlights and emergency flashers of six vehicles—Border Patrol cars and a Border Patrol van blocked both lanes of the road. Gus stopped the car and rolled down his window to ask what was wrong. But the Border Patrolman and his companion did not reply; instead, the first officer ordered us to "step out of the car." Gus asked why we had to get out of the car. His question seemed to set them off—two more Border Patrolmen immediately approached the car and one of them asked, "Are you looking for trouble?" as if he would relish the opportunity. Like other U.S. law enforcement officers, Border Patrolmen feel that if a citizen asks a question or at any time speaks when not spoken to, the citizen is being disorderly.

I will never forget that night beside the highway. There was an awful feeling of menace and of violence straining to break loose. It was clear that they would be happy to drag us out of the car if we did not comply. So we both got out of the car and they motioned for us to stand on the shoulder of the road. The night was very dark, and no other traffic had come down the road since they had stopped us. I thought how easy it would be for the Border Patrolmen to shoot us and leave our bodies and car beside the road. There were two other Border Patrolmen by the van. The man who had asked if we were looking for trouble told his partner to "get the dog," and from the back of the white van another Border Patrolman brought a small female German shepherd on a leash. The dog did not heel well enough to suit him, and I saw the dog's handler jerk the leash. They opened the doors of our car and pulled the dog's head into the car, but I saw immediately from the expression in her eyes that the dog hated them, and she would not serve them. When she showed no interest in the inside of the car, they brought her around back to the trunk near where we were standing. They half-dragged her up into the trunk, but still she did not indicate stowed-away humans or illegal drugs.

Their mood got uglier; they seemed outraged that the dog could not find any contraband, and they dragged her over to us and commanded her to sniff our legs and feet. To my relief, the strange anger the INS agents had focused at us now had shifted to the dog. I no longer felt so strongly that we would be murdered. We exchanged looks—the dog and I. She was afraid of what they might do, just as I was. The handler jerked the leash violently as she sniffed us, as if to make her perform better, but the dog refused to accuse us. The dog had an innate dignity, an integrity that did not permit her to serve those men. I can't forget the expression in her eyes; it was as if she was embarrassed to be associated with them. I had a small amount of prescription marijuana in my purse that night, but the dog refused to expose me. I am not partial to dogs, but I can't forget the small German shepherd. She saved us from the strange murderous mood of the Border Patrolmen that night.

In February of 1993, I was invited by the Women's Studies Department at UCLA to be a distinguished visiting lecturer. After I had described my run-ins with the Border Patrol, a professor of history at UCLA related her story. It seems she had been traveling by train from Los Angeles to Albuquerque twice each month to work with an informant. She had noticed that the Border Patrol officers were there each week to meet the Amtrak trains to scrutinize the passengers, but since she is six feet tall and of Irish and German ancestry, she was not particularly concerned. Then one day when she stepped off the train in Albuquerque, two Border Patrolmen accosted her. They wanted to know what she was doing, why she was traveling between Los Angeles and Albuquerque. This is the sort of police state that has developed in the southwest United States. No person, no citizen is free to travel without the scrutiny of the Border Patrol. Because Reverend Fife and the sanctuary movement brings political refugees into the United States from Central America, the Border Patrol is suspicious of and detains white people who appear to be clergy, those who wear ethnic clothing or jewelry, and women who wear very long hair or very short hair (they could be nuns). Men with beards and men with long hair are also likely to be detained because INS agents suspect "those sorts" of white people may help political refugees.

In Phoenix the INS agents raid public high schools and drag dark-skinned students away to their vans. In 1992, in El Paso, Texas, a high school football coach driving a vanload of his players in full uniform was pulled over on the freeway and INS agents put a cocked revolver to the coach's head through the van window. That incident was one of many similar abuses by the INS in the El Paso area that finally resulted in a restraining order against the Border Patrol issued by a federal judge in El Paso.

At about the same time, a Border Patrol agent in Nogales shot an unarmed undocumented immigrant in the back one night and attempted to hide the body; a few weeks earlier the same Border Patrol agent had shot and wounded another undocumented immigrant. His fellow agent, perhaps realizing Agent Elmer had gone around the bend, refused to help in the cover-up, so Agent Elmer threatened to kill him. Agent Elmer was arrested and tried for murder, but his southern Arizona jury empathized with his fear of brown-skinned people; they believed Agent Elmer's story that he feared for his life even though the victim was shot in the back trying to flee. Agent Elmer was also cleared of the charges of wounding in the other case. For years, undocumented immigrant women have reported sexual assaults by Border Patrol agents. But it wasn't until Agent Elmer was tried for murder that another Nogales INS agent was convicted of the rape of a woman he had taken into custody for detainment. In the city of South Tucson, where 80 percent of the respondents were Chicano or Mexicano, a research project by the University of Wisconsin recently revealed that one out of every five persons living there had been stopped by INS agents in the past year.

I no longer feel the same about driving from Tucson to Albuquerque via the southern route. For miles before I approach the INS check stations, I can feel the anxiety pressing hard against my chest. But I feel anger, too, a deep, abiding anger at the U.S. government, and I know that I am not alone in my hatred of these racist immigration policies, which are broadcast every day, teaching racism, demonizing all people of color, labeling indigenous people from Mexico as "aliens"—creatures not quite human.

The so-called civil wars in El Salvador and Guatemala are actually wars against the indigenous tribal people conducted by the white and mestizo ruling classes. These are genocidal wars conducted to secure Indian land once and for all. The Mexican government is buying Black Hawk helicopters in preparation for the eradication of the Zapatistas after the August elections.

I blame the U.S. government—congressmen and senators and President Clinton. I blame Clinton most of all for playing the covert racism card marked "Immigration Policy." The elected officials, blinded by greed and ambition, show great disrespect to the electorate they represent. The people, the ordinary people in the street, evidence only a fraction of the racist behavior that is exhibited on a daily basis by the elected leaders of the United States and their sluttish handmaidens, the big television networks.

If we truly had a representative democracy in the United States, I do not think we would see such a shameful level of racism in this country. But so long as huge amounts of money are necessary in order to run for office, we will not have a representative democracy. The form of government we have in the United States right now is not representative democracy but "big capitalism"; big capitalism can't survive for long in the United States unless the people are divided among themselves into warring factions. Big capitalism wants the people of the United States to blame "foreigners" for lost jobs and declining living standards so the people won't place the blame where it really belongs: with our corrupt U.S. Congress and president.

As I prepare to drive to New Mexico this week, I feel a prickle of anxiety down my spine. Only a few years ago, I used to travel the highways between Arizona and New Mexico with a wonderful sensation of absolute freedom as I cruised down the open road and across the vast desert plateaus in southern Arizona and southern New Mexico. We citizens of the United States grew up believing this freedom of the open road to be our inalienable right. The freedom of the open road meant we could travel freely from state to state without special papers or threat of detainment; this was a "right" citizens of Communist and totalitarian governments did not possess. That wide open highway was what told us we were U.S. citizens. Indeed, some say, this freedom to travel is an integral part of the American identity.

To deny this right to me, to some of us who because of skin color or other physical characteristics "appear" to fit fictional profiles of "undesirables," is to begin the inexorable slide into further government-mandated "race policies" that can only end in madness and genocide. The slaughters in Rwanda and Bosnia did not occur spontaneously—with neighbor butchering neighbor out of the blue; no, politicians and government officials called down these maelstroms of blood on their people by unleashing the terrible irrational force which racism is.

Take a drive down Interstate 8 or Interstate 10, along the U.S.-Mexico border. Notice the Border Patrol checkpoints all vehicles must pass through. When the Border Patrol agent asks you where you are coming from and where you are going, don't kid around and answer in Spanish—you could be there all afternoon. Look south into Mexico and enjoy the view while you are still able, before you find yourself behind the twelve-foot steel "curtain" the U.S. government is building.

john edgar wideman

john
edgar
wideman

John Edgar Wideman, born in 1941, is the author of more than a dozen works of fiction and nonfiction. His novels include *A Glance Away, Hurry Home, The Lynchers, Hiding Place, Sent For You Yesterday, Reuben*, and *Philadelphia Fire*. Wideman is the author of two volumes of short stories and an acclaimed memoir, *Brothers and Keepers*. His most recent book, *Fatheralong: A Meditation on Fathers and Sons, Race and Society*, was a finalist for the National Book Award. A Rhodes scholar, Wideman received the 1984 PEN/Faulkner Award, the 1984 Dos Passos Prize for Literature, and a MacArthur Fellowship.

John Edgar Wideman, not unlike James Baldwin, has told the many-layered story of his family with such open-faced honesty that it has become one of the primary testimonies of our time. His account of his journey to the South with his father, in *Fatheralong*, delivers a shattering picture of American racial history, at the same time that it brings a father and son together.

Wideman is a professor of English at the University of Massachusetts, in Amherst.

father stories

Perhaps it's inevitable. The hairline receding, the stone rolled back, the need to peer into the tomb of what's happened and yet to happen, to imagine yourself entering, then returning, the conversations you might have had with your father, if he could have spoken, if you had been ready to listen to whatever he might have said. My friend Mike nods his head. Boy. I wish I had the chance now, you know. He says the words slowly, pauses between words, staring away from me into the emptiness shrouding his dead father when I tell him I'm thinking about traveling to Pittsburgh then South Carolina for the long-delayed conversations with mine.

Age brings you to your father. You are much older now than he was in your earliest memory of him, old enough to be the father of the man he was that day in Pittsburgh, snow falling, the downtown sidewalks crowded with parade watchers, your father a young man lifting you to his shoulder so you can peer over other people's heads into the cleared space where the marchers will appear, a space yawning and vacant and unaccountably frightening, it would swallow you, you'd sizzle and disappear like a water drop in a hot skillet if you stepped out there. You cannot fathom how this broad, empty avenue you wouldn't dare cross will bear the weight of everything you expect to fill it any second, contain the parade you've been waiting hours for, the memory of it ancient before it arrives.

You recall snow and it may have been snowing that cold afternoon in Pittsburgh waiting for a parade, but none of it sticks, it dissolves as swiftly on the streets as it does when you tilt your face up to find the snow's source. When you think no one is looking, you open your mouth, sneak out your tongue, and the nothing taste of snow disappoints you, another wet blot barely lasts long enough on your eyelash to flick away.

Snow seems part of that afternoon, falling perhaps early in the day and stopping before the parade commences, or a damp raw chill in the air the whole time you are standing watching, then flurries gradually more visible until the parade's scraggly tail end approaches, then larger and larger white flakes swirl around the marchers, the spectators, flakes beginning to settle, to cover the streets of the parade route, the entire downtown disappearing under a blanket of whiteness, everything quiet and gone without a trace as the trolley you ride with your mother carries you through darkening streets home.

Snow part of the earliest memory of my father whether it was falling that day or not, snow frames the picture, a stylized presence at the edges, a curtain I brush aside to enter, a silence shutting again behind my back as I depart, snow and the certainty I am wrapped in many layers of clothes, my mother would have overdressed me for the winter day and trip downtown, the normal gravity of how it felt to stand with my own two feet on the sidewalk absent. Boots, snowsuit, mittens sweater flannel shirt bibbed corduroy trousers undershirt two pairs of socks a cap hood and scarf muffled me, bloated me, made me an astronaut long before anybody had walked on the moon, a deep-sea diver just this side of the bends after my father snatches me from the ocean floor to the promontory of his shoulder. I believe snow fell that day and know I was dressed for the Arctic. Know I snuggled up to my mother and slept during the long trolley ride home from downtown, though my only proof of these things is this memory of snow the day I'm constructing almost fifty years later, letting pieces float into place as I know they must have, tilting my head back again to find the hole in the sky where everything comes from.

I know my father is not on the trolley my mother and I ride home from the Thanksgiving Day parade. I'm asleep, tired from the long, full day that started for me before dawn, lying awake listening for the first sounds of my mother up. The room still dark as I drift free of sleep, anticipating her bare feet slapping the floor, her trip to pee, imagining what the day might bring, exhausting myself trying to name things that might happen, wanting to be asleep again so I could hurry up and wake up again in the middle of everybody's preparations to go. The kind of restless, excited morning alone in bed remembering times when all I'd need to drop peacefully asleep would be my mother's body, her warmth, the sound and smell of her, her hand stroking my hair, folding me closer into her sleep, a sleep she doesn't need to break to let me in. Tired long before the day started for anyone else so I lean into her, drift, melt, the charmed circle of her arm around my shoulders hugging me while the trolley sways and clomps like the old ice-wagon horse over broken streets.

My father would not be on the trolley because he goes on to another job after his downtown-morning-till-late-afternoon gig in the restaurant of Kaufmann's Department Store. I visited him once on the top floor of Kaufmann's, waiting for hours it seemed, anxious to be noticed and not noticed, till one of the brown men in white jackets asked me if I was Eddie's son and smiled at me when I nodded and mumbled Yessir. He said, Just a minute, sonny, you sit down right here just a minute. I'll fetch your daddy. My father's buddy Chooky, Chooky Bolden whose name I wouldn't have heard for years until my mother said it to someone, "poor man drank himself to death, passed out and froze to death in his own driveway." Chooky Bolden snatched the used white cloth from the table where he'd seated me, folding it while it *still* floated in the air, tucking it under one arm as he produced another from somewhere and unfurled it, whiter, brighter, snapping it like a shoeshine rag so it spread and hovered a split second before settling over the round tabletop. With more hands than anyone I'd ever seen, he continued doing three or four things simultaneously. In an instant plates, saucers, cups, glasses, silverware, salt and pepper shakers, menus, and napkins red as the restaurant rug were arranged before me. Eddie be here soon as he can. Been busy as a bee's nest in here. Bout got it whipped now. Crackers be clearing out lickety-split. How you doing today, sonny? You're a fine-looking young man. Look just like your daddy. Said all at once and too quickly for me to reply even if I'd known what I was supposed to say back to the brown-skinned man in his black pants and gleaming white jacket who was gone before I could be sure he'd been standing there in front of me, loading and unloading the skinny cart he wheeled away before I could open my mouth. Or shut it. Chooky Bolden who took our orders, served my father and me in our corner of a restaurant of white people with a kind of seamless efficiency, always present but unseen till we needed something, there and not there, invisible as I hoped we were to the other diners, invisible as they were to me from our corner table because I kept my eyes on my plate or on my father's face the whole time we ate. Pretending the white people weren't there was a way of keeping them from bothering us, protecting the precious, private time with my father.

Having lunch with me at a white-topped table served by Chooky Bolden was not my father's job. I was afraid they'd summon him away any minute to do his job, and I'd be left alone. If I could have, I would have held on to some part of him the whole time, wrist or ankle or hooked my arm around his neck. But he was not in the trolley. In addition to waiting tables at Kaufmann's he worked at two different clubs Monday through Thursday and many private parties weekends. I couldn't keep up with where he was nights or which hours he was supposed to be home. I just knew better than to bother him because he might be asleep any hour of the day.

Five days a week, roughly during school hours, if I thought of my father, I could place him in the dining room of Kaufmann's Department Store. After my visit I could place myself there also, keeping out of people's way, avoiding the eyes of anybody who might ask me my business, ask me what business did I have hanging around a restaurant only grown white people entered and left, what business did I have slipping past the hostess and the little brass pole with a tasseled rope attached she lowered and raised to regulate traffic. At my desk in school I could see myself spying on the waiters in short white jackets and black pants, needing one to be my father, trying to guess which one, afraid my father's face, like mine when I ventured into unknown places, might change. He'd be wearing different features when he waited tables at Kaufmann's and I'd never find him.

So I did not expect him to ride the trolley home with us from the parade. I didn't expect him to do much more than come and go like a ghost, at odd hours, to sleep, to eat, to meet me that one time on his job when I stepped off the elevator to have lunch with him and go to a movie, the two of us alone for once. He was my father and worked long and hard for us. We slept in the same house but at different hours. He was around or not around according to a schedule I couldn't fathom but believed unfair. I learned to accept things as they were, not to expect more, learned as kids must, the only way around powerlessness is to make up stuff, to cheat, steal, lie.

In the house on Copeland Street in Shadyside we lived on the second floor. My mother and father slept in a closet-sized room at the end of the hall on the landing above the front-door stairs. With no particular reason to be sneaky, other than I definitely didn't want anyone else to know what I was doing, I'd stand in my parents' room when it was empty or sit in the hall outside their door those odd weekend daylight times when the rest of us were up but my father was still inside the room snoring away.

Why these were secret times, times I felt vaguely ashamed of then and still do, I can't exactly say. Perhaps the secret had something to do with my father's smell, seeping off his body while he slept, in his clothes, the sheets and blankets when he wasn't in the room. A smell inseparable from the fact he was larger, stronger, darker, that he occupied lots of space, owned it, stamped it even when he wasn't around. Not stink exactly, but the funk of maleness, his work, his sweat and breathing, his comings and goings when the rest of us weren't awake, him staying out all night if he wanted to, or sleeping all day, his power to leave the house, to raise his voice and punish us whether we deserved it or not, to fill the room, the bed he shared with my mother, to shit and shave first in the bathroom, singing while the rest of us waited, scuffling Sunday mornings to get ready for church. Not exactly stink but a threat of nastiness in the scent he marked things with. Pungent nastiness I envied and feared because it defined something about my person, too, something he'd pass on to me, the sign of myself clinging to me as he clings to him, a cause when I was around other people of deep shame and embarrassment, a source when I was alone of bottomless curiosity.

I breathed him in and it was like stealing, like unwrapping an edge of one of those silver-foil packets he brought home from jobs and pinching nibbles from the delicacies whose names I didn't know, often didn't like the salty taste of, but needed to pry open and sample anyway, even at the risk of my father's wrath, trespassing perhaps because I wanted to get caught, wanted to trigger my father's anger, the real thing when he'd snatch me or shake me or yell at me then fix me in a glare that said, Boy, something awful's going to happen to you, happen with no mercy, no escape, so terrible I need a minute to figure out just how I'm going to arrange it. Maybe what I hoped to get when I dug into the booty he liberated from the fancy parties he served was a taste of him, even if it had to take the form of an angry exchange, it would be preferable to opening the refrigerator and finding the shiny package gone. Preferable to waiting for the other kind of anger, trumped-up, secondhand, when he was less mad at me than at my mother for setting him up to be the executioner after he dragged in from work because I'd acted up during the day and she'd laid down the wait-till-your-father-gets-home threat for him to make good and he has to tighten his lips and coax the chill into his eyes and hurt me enough so I swear I'll never do it again, never do it again.

Learning his odor, fixing it in my mind, the same way I made it my business to bumble around with every sense hyperalert in rooms in my grandmother's house in Finance Street where women were dressing or undressing or relaxing, not dressed in much at all, me not seeming to pay any attention to them and too young anyway, they thought, to be thinking much about the parts of them different than my parts. Sometimes one of my aunts or my mother would call me over, smile, pat me on the head, and I'd see bare breasts or brush against something soft or naked it would take me years to see again or touch again on some other live female body, some other soft sweet tune playing for me in love or not in love in a different fashion with the bare flesh I touched or watched later. A different kind of intimacy years later but also returning me to the wonder and bonding of those early, easy times with my aunts and mother when I was a spy, a fly on the wall of warm, scented rooms in which they dressed and undressed, chatting with each other, casual in their bodies, unsuspicious or not caring or benignly silent about everything bad they understood about me better than I knew myself, letting me disappear as they busied themselves with the things women do together, do alone.

On the trolley my mother's saying something to me but I hear only singsong nicknames, baby prattle, nothing in her voice I can't draw down with me into the place where I'm pretending not to be awake. She's fishing for me with little bright bobbing teasing lures, coaxing me out of the deep pocket of her where I'm hiding. C'mon you. I know you're not asleep. She's not playing now, not singing. I cannot remember precisely how, but I could tell from the feel of the trolley when we had arrived in Homewood. I knew, even though I possessed no words then or now to say it precisely, how riding a trolley through Homewood was different than riding it anywhere else. You'd know even if you were blind. The side-to-side pitch or jolts, the rhythm of stop and go. You wouldn't need eyes to see the Homewood people, the Homewood buildings, or ears to hear Homewood voices. Riding along with your eyes squeezed shut and hands over your ears you could feel the steep inclines, the sharp curves, a long smooth glide at the bend of Frankstown Avenue, Hamilton's cobblestones chattering your teeth. So I knew why my mother had stopped singing. Why she pulled away so I had to balance myself upright on the trolley seat's hard weave. My own backbone and backside responsible again inside the bundle of clothes she'd made me wear to the parade. We were home again.

The walk from the trolley stop on Hamilton Avenue to my grandmother's house on Finance Street is not far, only five or six short blocks, but also for years much farther than I was allowed to venture on my own. So that evening, after the parade, and nights years later when I'm out prowling for women or mischief or both and cross Hamilton, it registered as a boundary, a line dividing my turf from unknown territory. Walking, probably with my hand in my mother's, through dark, empty, snow-dusted streets from the trolley stop home the night of the parade I knew exactly what was waiting for me. The streets were like the bulky clothing I wore, not me, maybe even a little cumbersome, unnecessary, but I felt comfortable and protected inside them and understood that in a few minutes I'd be free of them, home, relaxing, getting ready for bed. The same short passage, the same walk on Dunfermline past the same houses and trees and street corners, changed if you were going from Finance to Hamilton, the opposite direction, away from home rather than toward home. Then you were approaching the edge, you didn't wear the streets, they rode your back, giddy-up, go, go, go on, boy, urging you to cross Hamilton and get into whatever was over there, what wasn't tamed or predictable, whatever made those streets, those rungs climbing the ladder of Bruston Hill—Kelly, Sterett, Braddock, Frankstown—different and forbidden till you were grown enough to know better, or think you did, and not give a good goddamn.

Beyond Hamilton you might run into your father. I wouldn't have thought that then. But my mother did, her sisters and her mother did, so somehow the knowledge must have been part of me, learned as I learned most things, not only because of what the women said, but because I also studied the school of their bodies, how they moved, their silences, the animation of hands and lips and eyes, touching, guiding, freeing my flesh. They practiced on me as if I could be all the men they'd ever known or wished they'd known or cared to know: Don't you wish his granddaddy was here today to see him. Daddy'd be so proud, he'd bust a gut. This boy's his father all over again. Look at those bedroom eyes. Trouble for some poor gal someday. I'm glad he got at least a taste of his father's color. Nothing more handsome than a good-looking dark brown-skinned man. Horton's color. Yes, indeed.

Horton Moon was a handsome dog in his day. Still is if he'd stop wearing that Afro wig. More dog than handsome in that black, good-for-nothing nigger. Whoa. If he drove up today in that three-tone green Buick Riviera and tooted his horn, you'd knock us down, girl, getting out to the curb. I'd tell you something else knock you down if Mr. Bigears wasn't sitting over in the corner taking everything in. And then Aunt Catherine Moon would cut her eyes and do something with one shoulder, shrugging something off or pumping herself up or hinting at some dance move memorized long ago and buried deep in nerves and muscles, a slight hitch, twitch, jerk, snap, dip of one shoulder releases her entire body, lightens her, raises her on her toes so whatever else she's doing, wherever she happens to be, she is also for a sixteenth of a second twenty-one years old again and dancing in the South Park Pavilion to Jeeps Blues. Or the gesture means something else entirely I can only guess at, amazed how the mystery both unravels and deepens. Will the same gesture another time, another place, another woman performing it, teach me more? Whatever it meant, she felt better after doing it and I loved it and it registered as a whole story about Aunt Catherine, my father's sister. She was okay, all right, fine, no matter what foolishness or hurt came before or followed the gesture. She was fine. Flashed her power then locked it up again with those other resources she could bring to bear on what might be unmanageable otherwise.

If I sensed I might run into my father, over there in the disreputable, darker streets of Homewood, then crossing Hamilton must have been a way of seeking him. Not his person, but all the power and privilege I associated with his person. Built into the seeking were also many levels of betrayal. I was betraying the women who lived in my grandmother's house on Finance, the confidences they'd shared with me, their confidence in me. What in the world could I be looking for across Hamilton, except the precise dangers the women had organized their lives, with great cost to themselves, to protect me from. Painstakingly organized their dress and speech, their manner of comporting themselves in public, organized their church, its music and prayers and Sunday school and upright deacons, who'd managed like the women in my family to stay off the far end of Homewood Avenue, the nastiness flourishing there we'd see the tail of sometimes as it straggled up past the church from Hamilton Avenue, unwashed, shameless, high as a kite, loud and oblivious on a Sunday morning. Like it was any old morning. Pointing, teasing, laughing at us dressed in our Sunday best as we're hustled into the church's side door by some scandalized, fit-to-be-tied adult. I could toss all the women's sacrifices out the window simply by putting my foot on the wrong path at the wrong time. Once. Betrayal was loss of respect for them, their struggle on my behalf, the one they'd died for a little bit, to raise a little bit higher, the one into whose hands they'd chanced so much of themselves that disrespecting myself would also be bringing them down.

Did the prospect of finding my father over there beyond Hamilton put my flight in a different light? Not so much deserting or shaming the women, as it was seeking him. Loyalty the flip side of betrayal. If and when I found him, would he punish me for being in the wrong place, doing the wrong thing, punish me or welcome me or instruct me how to run farther, how to find my way home again.

Whatever I caught him doing or he caught me doing in the bars or poolroom or sitting on the porch steps of a houseful of pretty women or standing on the corner working out schemes to get off the goddamn same ole shit corner, schemes you couldn't forge or discuss anywhere except on the corner and therefore schemes keeping your ass nailed to the corner day after day working out details, wherever we bumped into each other I hoped the flash of light when he recognized and spoke to me would be bright enough, the music loud enough to drown the sound of walls tumbling, the women shaking their heads and dropping their eyes in embarrassment and disappointment. Lost in some joint in Frankstown where I'd dragged them to look for my daddy.

Betraying him, too. Because seeking him in the bars, the streets over there beyond Hamilton, I was confirming the women's version of him. Searching for proof, trying to catch him red-handed. The part of me that was him, part of the evidence against him. My guilt proved his, his proved mine. Out there carrying on just like your father Tattletale proof in the pudding.

On the other hand, there was always the chance I might learn something new, something the women neglected to tell me, didn't know, couldn't know since they'd never hung out in the places where my father went nights. Maybe I could bring back glad tidings. Maybe I could come and go between my mother's world and my father's world, close the gap separating them.

But a spy couldn't be an emissary, couldn't pretend to be a proper spy until he figured out whom he was serving, where his loyalties finally resided, and that question was irresolvable, remains so this instant.

The first rule of my father's world is that you stand alone. Alone, alone, alone. A fact about which we have no choice or say, carved in stone above the portal we enter when we arrive on this earth. Your work in the world is to grasp this truth, never lose sight of it, turn it so it catches light from all angles, squeeze it till its hardness, its intractability is alchemied into a source of strength. Accept the bottom line, icy clarity of the one thing you can rely on: nothing. Your power, your work is to exempt yourself from illusion, handle yourself, conduct your business without ever forgetting who and what you can count on: nothing. You are proud when you don't let yourself forget and always wind up regretting your slips, those occasions when you compromise, when you let go of the truth even for a second, even in the smallest exchanges with the few people you allow a smidgen closer to you than you allow everyone else. You are, if you're my father, calculating, relentless, disciplined beyond belief in adhering to this self-imposed regimen. Not because it brings happiness or satisfaction in the usual sense. You don't expect to make things better. You don't do what you do in order to produce consequences anywhere but within your own skull, on the meter toting up your hardheaded power to deny, to withdraw, to remain detached. What counts is the doing, the discipline, the engagement with nothing on its own terms.

My mother's first rule was love. She refused to believe she was alone. *Be not dismayed, whate'er betides / God will take care of you.* The nothing my father acknowledged was for her just as cold and hard and unbearable a truth, but it could not encroach beyond a circle she drew in the air around herself. Her God's arms were that circle and he was also inside with her. Think of circling arms. My mother's arms around her children, her grandkids, her sisters and brother, nephews and nieces, and inside that circle of family, smaller circles, two bodies clinging, five or six in a tight huddle, circles concentric, overlapping, intertwined, generations long gone and yet to be born connected indivisibly. The first circle a pinpoint of affection gleaming in a child's eye, the last a radiant, all-encompassing arc, the great mother or great father's embrace. Unbroken circles expanding, contracting, rainbow circles you can visualize an instant if you don the mask of Damballah, hold all time, Great Time in your unflinching gaze.

Think of thread spun finer than silk but steel-strong, stronger, much stronger as it stretches, loops, weaves, webs. The yawning void, nothingness stopped outside the ring of love. A fingertip pressing against yours with the resolution, the determination not to lose touch becomes a fence against the nothing.

Love the work, love the power in my mother's world. You are not alone unless you let go of love, and if you let go, then you truly are nothing.

I couldn't maintain a foot in both worlds. The stretch was too great. Neither Father's son nor Mother's son, betraying them both as I became myself. My mother's open arms. My father's arms crossed on his chest.

I hope this is not a hard day for you. I hope you can muster peace within yourself and deal with the memories, the horrors of the past seven years. It must strike you as strange, as strange as it strikes me, that seven years have passed already. I remember a few days after hearing you were missing and a boy found dead in the room the two of you had been sharing, I remember walking down toward the lake to be alone because I felt myself coming apart, the mask I'd been wearing, as much for myself as for the benefit of other people, was beginning to splinter. I could hear ice cracking great rents and seams breaking my face into pieces, carrying away chunks of numb flesh. I found myself on my knees, praying to a tree. In the middle of some absurdly compelling ritual I'd forgotten I carried the memory of. Yet there I was on my knees, digging my fingers into the loose soil, grabbing up handfuls, sinking my face into the clawed earth as if it might heal. Speaking to the roots of a pine tree as if its shaft might carry my message up to the sky, send it on its way to whoever I thought my anguish should be addressed.

I was praying to join you. Offering myself in exchange for you. Take me. Take me. Free my son from the terrible things happening to him. Take me in his place. Let them happen to me, I was afraid you were dying or already dead or suffering unspeakable tortures at the hands of a demon kidnapper. The tears I'd held back were flowing finally, a flood that brought none of the relief I must have believed hoarding them would earn me when I let go at last. Just wetness burning, clouding my eyes. I couldn't will the spirit out of my body into the high branches of that tree. What felt familiar, felt like prayers beside my bed as a child, or church people moaning in the amen corner, or my mother weeping and whispering *hold on, hold on* to herself as she rocks side to side and mourns, or some naked priest chanting and climbing toward the light on a bloody ladder inside his chest, these memories of what might have been visions of holiness could not change the simple facts. I was a man who most likely had lost his son, and hugging trees and burying his face in dirt and crying for help till breath slunk out of his body wouldn't change a thing.

A desperate, private moment, one of thousands I could force myself to dredge up if I believed it might serve some purpose. I share that one example with you to say the seven years have not passed quickly.

The years are countless moments, many as intense as this one I'm describing to you, moments I conceal from myself as I've hidden them from other people. Other moments, also countless, when terrible things had to be shared, spoken aloud, in phone calls with lawyers, depositions, interviews, conferences, in the endless conversations with your mother. Literally endless because often the other business of our lives would seem merely a digression from the dialogue with you, about you. A love story finally, love of you, your brother and sister, since no word except love makes sense of the ever-present narrative our days unfold.

Time can drag like a long string, studded and barbed, through a fresh wound so it hasn't gone quickly. The moment-to-moment, day-by-day struggles imprint my flesh, but the seven years also a miracle, a blink of the eye through which I watch myself wending my way from there to here. In this vast house of our fathers and mothers.

Your mother didn't need my words or images to work out her grief. She needed time. Took the time she needed to slowly, gradually, painstakingly unravel feelings knotted in what seemed for a while a hopeless tangle. No choice really. She's who she is. Can give nothing less than her whole heart to you, to this place inseparable from all our lives her father, your grandfather, provided.

For a while I guess it must have felt impossible. And still can, I know. She may have doubted her strength, her capacity to give enough, give everything because everything seemed to be tearing her apart, breaking her down. She needed time. Not healing time exactly, since certain wounds never heal, but time to change and more time to learn to believe, to understand she could go on, was going on for better or worse. She could be someone she'd never dreamed she could be. Her heart strong, whole, even as it cracks and each bit demands everything.

The fullness of time. The fullness of time. That phrase has haunted me since I first heard it or read it, though I don't know when or how the words entered my awareness, because they seem always to have been there, like certain melodies, for instance, or visual harmonies of line in your mother's body, I wonder how I've ever lived without, the first time I encountered them, although another recognition clicked in almost simultaneously, reminding me that I'd been waiting for those particular notes, those lines, a very long time. They'd been forming me before I formed my first impression of them.

The fullness of time. Neither forward nor backward. A space capacious enough to contain your coming into and going out of the world, your consciousness of these events, the wrap of oblivion bedding them. A life, the passage of a life, the truest understanding, measure, experience of time's fullness. So many lives and each different, each unknowable, no matter how similar to yours, your flesh and not your flesh, lives passing, as yours, into the fullness of time, where each of these lives and all of them together make no larger ripple than yours, all and each abiding in the unruffled innocence of the fullness that is time. All the things that mattered so much to you or them sinking into a dreadful, unfeatured equality that is also rest and peace, time gone but more always more, the hands writing, the hands snatching, hands becoming bones then dust then whatever comes next, what time takes and fashions of you after the possibilities, permutations and combinations, the fullness in you is exhausted, played out for the particular shape it's assumed for a time in you, for you, you are never it, but what it could be, then is not, you not lost but ventured, gained, stretched, more, until the dust is particles and the particles play unhindered, unbound, returned to the fullness of time.

I know my father's name, Edgar, and some of his fathers' names, *Hannibal, Tatum, Jordan*, but I can't go back any farther than a certain point, except I also know the name of a place, Greenwood, South Carolina, and an even smaller community, Promised Land, nearly abutting Greenwood, where my grandfather, who's of course your great-grandfather, was born, and many of his brothers are buried there under sturdy tombstones bearing his name, our name, *Wideman* carved in stone in the place where the origins of the family name begin to dissolve into the loam of plantations owned by white men, where my grandfathers' identities dissolve, where they were boys, then men, and the men they were fade into a set of facts, sparse, ambiguous, impersonal, their intimate lives unretrievable, where what is known about a county, a region, a country and its practice of human bondage, its tradition of obscuring, stealing, or distorting black people's lives, begins to crowd out the possibility of seeing my ancestors as human beings. The powers and principalities that originally restricted our access to the life free people naturally enjoy still rise like a shadow, a wall between my grandfathers and myself, my father and me, between the two of us, father and son, son and father.

So we must speak stories to one another.

Love.

the *hungry mind* race questionnaire

Following is a list of simple and not-quite-so-simple questions on the subject of race in America.

1. How was race explained to you as a child? Was it explained to you at all?

2. What messages did your parents communicate to you about race issues?

3. How does this differ from the way you communicate with your children about race?

4. What are your most basic fears about race?

5. What is your race?

6. How important is race to your sense of self?

7. In what ways do you organize your identity and resources around race? How consciously does race affect your choice of where to live, shop, or send your children to school?

8. What would be the ideal percentage breakdown for you between people of your race and of others in a neighborhood in which you lived? What is the actual percentage breakdown in your neighborhood? What would be the "tipping point,"

the point at which the racial balance became uncomfortable enough to make you want to leave the neighborhood?

9. How do you account for the fact that the distribution of wealth among whites, blacks, and Native Americans is nearly the same now as it was in 1866, as slavery formally came to an end?

10. Is affirmative action an appropriate way of redressing racial inequities in this country?

11. Should whites in America think of themselves as a race?

12. How have your views about race and your own position in the racial scheme of things changed in the last ten years?

13. How did the O. J. Simpson case affect your sense of the American racial landscape?

14. What do you see as the dangers or positive effects of ethnocentricity, such as Eurocentricity or Afrocentricity?

15. What does the old concept of America as a melting pot mean to you?

16. What considerations should affect our immigration policies? Do you think we should place an equal quota on the immigration of Croats, Haitians, Canadians, Mexicans, Russians, Chinese, Somalians, Swedes, Palestinians?

17. What are your hopes and fears for a multiracial America?

18. What questions would you add to this list?